THE USES OF GOTHIC

D1568150

PLANNING AND BUILDING

THE USES OF GOTHIC

THE CAMPUS OF THE UNIVERSITY OF CHICAGO

1892-1932

JEAN F. BLOCK

THE UNIVERSITY OF CHICAGO PRESS

*Cover: Detail of a 360 degree panoramic
view of the campus from the center of the
main quadrangle, ca. 1903.*

O
L D
934
.B57
1983

This volume was first published in conjunction with the exhibition "The Uses of Gothic: Planning and Building the Campus of the University of Chicago, 1892–1932," held in The Joseph Regenstein Library, May through September, 1983. Support for that publication was received from friends of the University and the University of Chicago Library Society.

Library of Congress Catalog Card Number: 83-6545

The University of Chicago Library, Chicago 60637

©1983 by The University of Chicago Library.
All rights reserved.
Published 1983
University of Chicago Press edition 1984

Printed in the United States of America
ISBN 0-226-06004-7

DABNEY LANCASTER LIBRARY
LONGWOOD COLLEGE
FARMVILLE, VIRGINIA 23901

To the Trustees

who have generously given their time, talent, and judgment to planning the campus of

the University of Chicago

DABNEY LANCASTER LIBRARY

1000117349

TABLE OF CONTENTS

FOREWORD

According to most dictionaries "college campus" is an Americanism whose roots go back to the eighteenth century. Although word origins are not always trustworthy guides to cultural history there is a certain appropriateness to this one. For the college campus has long occupied a special status within the American landscape.

One reason is purely negative. It faced little competition. The youth, poverty, scale, and voluntarism of most American institutions argued against the construction of impressive ensembles, at least through the late nineteenth century. Few military, clerical, or fraternal foundations could dot the scene with the lavish structures and cultivated acreage they enjoyed in Europe. Castles, cathedrals, and fortresses were rarely met in the United States, and picturesque ruins were accessible only to tourists who journeyed back across the Atlantic, or south to Mexico and Central America.

The college campus took on special meaning for a second reason: the power of numbers. By the early nineteenth century the United States contained more colleges than several European countries combined. Religious convictions, state rivalries, and fears of cultural degeneration stimulated an unprecedented flurry of college creations. More than four hundred institutions were functioning when the University of Chicago was founded.

Of course claiming the title of college or university, like calling any motley collection of buildings and grounds a campus, could be an ambitious arrogation. Like city plans American campus schemes, even when born in grandiose hopes, usually collapsed into compromise and confusion. The conception Jefferson developed for the University of Virginia came early on the national scene, and it was never surpassed, setting a standard for later experiments. But the brilliant Charlottesville idea produced few imitators. However numerous their company or sentimental the loyalties they stimu-

lated, most American colleges grew by accretion. They rarely possessed either the money or the patience to work things out from the start.

Neither palatial nor quadrangular, departing from both the English and the Continental ideals, the American college featured rambling and often ill-defined grounds. Not without charm, particularly in small towns and country villages, campuses were peppered by lecture halls, Old Mains, pinnacled libraries, chapels, dormitories, and observatories. Writing with only measured sympathy about the old Harvard Yard in 1909, the architectural critic Montgomery Schuyler argued that the successive buildings were placed "wherever they would go without any thought whatsoever of their relation to one another. Neither in the ground plan nor in the actual aspect is there anything to be made out but higgledy-piggledy. There is no grouping, there are no vistas." Exceptions like Virginia, Union College in Schenectady, and Hartford's Trinity only emphasized the point more clearly.

Until the 1880s this was where things stood. But the changes which came in the following decade were as broad as they were sudden. Comprehensive schemes for Columbia, Berkeley, N.Y.U., Washington University, West Point, Stanford, and Chicago altered the university presence permanently. In 1888 James Bryce noted, almost parenthetically, that the new college buildings he had seen on his American trip were handsome and useful. He said little else about them. But by 1903, as *The Nation* pointed out in an editorial entitled "The College Beautiful," Bryce would have had to take more extended notice of the audacious plans under way. New institutions had the greatest scope, of course, but older colleges like Harvard, Yale, Penn, Amherst, Princeton, and Williams were also engaged in building extensive additions for themselves from the menu of Collegiate Gothic, Neo-Classic, and Renaissance forms offered them by their architects.

The American fin-de-siècle favored large plans. Encouragement for campus planning grew, as new landscapes multiplied. Besides Chicago's Columbian Exposition, a close neighbor to the University, there were huge fairs in Omaha, Buffalo, and St. Louis. These new fairs coincided with—and helped stimulate—massive new planning schemes for Cleveland, Chicago, San Francisco, Washington, D.C., Denver, and Minneapolis, most of them worked on after the century's end. There were the enormous new railroad stations like Grand Central and Pennsylvania in New York, Chicago's Northwestern and Washington's Union Station, along with impressive museums, libraries, hospitals, and office structures, all adding dramatic monumentality (and cloistered enclaves) to the national scene.

Some of this building activity between 1890 and 1910 bespoke the mere pressure of numbers and the stress of expansion. Rising population, changing technologies, and expanded transport required systematic ordering for minimal levels of efficiency and comfort. But the concern for landscaped harmony demonstrated something else, less specific but equally insistent, the intrusion of an aesthetic mandate. The haphazard, incongruous, and ill-fitting aspects of both city and countryside mocked the wealth and pretensions of many communities and appeared to threaten their stated ideals. In financial resources, size, and potential influence American institutions could compete with counterparts in Britain and Germany. Paintings, books, professors, even scholarly values were importable, to supplement what was already available. But until physical expression suited good taste and testified to permanence and cultural commitment, the institutions would be limited in their power. "Respect for the natural beauty and architectural possibility of its site is the measure of the culture of an institution," *The Nation* insisted. Seemly buildings displayed intellectuality "as plainly as dress betrays the wearer."

Many American colleges felt a lack of fit between purpose and posture in the 1890s. One source for the failure of American higher education to exert greater influence on contemporary life could be laid to the physical environment. Self-respect demanded scale and harmony. Architectural planning was no superfluity or costly luxury indulged only after other needs had been met. Expenditure and intelligent design were ways to cement loyalty and encourage those high principles that might counter the materialism that threatened community life. Progressive reformers, along a broad spectrum of interests, acknowledged with new enthusiasm the instrumental possibilities of the landscape.

The creation of Chicago's campus in the 1890s, then, was not anomalous. It fit squarely the new national concern for environmental effect. Special aspects of the Chicago scheme did add their own emphases. Jean Block outlines several: the conti-

nuity of the interested trustees; their need to assure potential supporters that this second University of Chicago would stay the course; the clarity of the English collegiate architecture which served as their model. But two features of the Chicago plan transcend particularity.

One concerned its immediate surroundings. The village of Hyde Park had been annexed by the city of Chicago just a couple of years before the University began. American universities would, increasingly, have close ties with, if not actual location in, large cities. But while it was *in* the city, the University of Chicago was not firmly *of* the city. Suburban in character, flat, unornamented, still largely treeless, its local landscape offered few scenic highlights. The one exception was the great lakefront, a short walk away. Jefferson's University of Virginia lay open at one end to the agreeable Virginia countryside, inviting its students and faculty to gaze out on a scene that, to Jefferson at least, summoned up the symbols of republican yeomanry. But this did not exist in Chicago. No Cam, no Isis, no Rhine, no Seine, no mountaintops or sacred groves beckoned to young scholars. The

University intended to provide its own landscape. Or at least it gave evidence that it would do so eventually.

The campus, therefore, began from its perimeters rather than its center, creating its boundaries and marking off its territory. In the first years this meant incongruities and strange separations. As Dean George E. Vincent explained in a 1902 magazine article, because of the presence of "a final plan, a few buildings may seem isolated, and here and there unfinished." The distances were sometimes more magnificent than the structures. But it meant also a certain degree of spaciousness, whatever the sacrifice of historic growth. As early as 1906 H. G. Wells could comment on the trees and green spaces, "a wonderful contrast to the dark congestions of the mercantile city of the north. To all the disorganization of that it is even physically antagonistic. . . ." Like many future institutions the University confronted its relationship to the outer world by emphasizing discontinuity rather than unhindered access. Despite the many ties that would develop to both the downtown and the urban netherworld, the campus would remain a place apart.

There were dangers here, of course. But also advantages. Viewing the walls and gates of another American campus in 1904 Henry James noted the way in which "the formal enclosure of objects at all interesting immediately refines upon their interest." It "establishes values." Creating such precincts resembled, in the social order, "the improved situation of the foundling who has discovered his family or of the actor who has mastered his part." In view of the growing importance of alumni ties and academic ceremonial, James's incorporation of domestic and theatrical imagery was prescient. The campus was a stage, and it needed its boundaries.

The other feature of Chicago's plan was its uniformity. Gothic permitted variation and idiosyncrasy but it set the general tone. In later years critics ranging from Thorstein Veblen to Upton Sinclair would pillory the strange spectacle of modern scientific research taking place within a medieval dream facade. The conjunction of gargoyles and test tubes seemed hard to accept. Yet the architectural homogeneity was in part a response to the new institution's bewildering diversity. Specialization of function, abstruseness of expertise, mutual incomprehension of scholarly inquirers bothered patrons and supporters who were seeking, in universities, unities to hold the social order together. With its dozens of departments, its professional schools, museums, preparatory divisions, publishing houses, and extension services the modern university challenged the energies of the most aggressive administrator. Gothic architecture—early, late, or middle—emerged as a symbol of reassurance for some of the era's most anxious critics. Fostering the style within a research university emphasized, as Jean Block points out, its priestly function, its mediating role. But it served also to remind each school and sector of its subordinate place within the larger setting.

In the subsequent history of the University of Chicago the theme of mutual dependence would be sounded by many presidents and deans, insisting that survival and prosperity required that professional and disciplinary ambitions be subordinated to the goals of the University as a whole. The campus stamped its parts with a single impress. A Cambridge University vice-chancellor, visiting after World War I, termed Chicago "one of the most complete and uniform of all American Universi-

ties," and found himself repeating the interpretation of the dramatic unities as Mr. Curdle explained them to Nicholas Nickleby, " 'a completeness—a kind of universal dovetailedness with regard to place and time—a sort of general oneness, if I may be allowed to use so strong an expression.' " Whether this unity resulted from the University "anticipating its own vastness," as the American journalist Julian Street put it about the same time, or simply reflected the conjunction of dream and opportunity, the result was to establish a strong sense of corporate self, within only a decade or two of the new foundation. The University of Chicago would never lose a sense of presence that gave it, even as a comparative newcomer, a special personality among the country's universities.

These two problems—connecting to the outer world and imposing some organizational ideal upon the inner structure—would be solved in various ways by colleges and universities in succeeding decades. Campuses expanding considerably in the 1950s, 60s, and 70s, would project different values and experiences. Chicago's Gothic campus presented only one approach, but that it exemplified. The survival of classic texts and a concern for the centrality and even fixity of form would, as it happened, become themes in the University's pedagogical and intellectual style during the twentieth century. The campus was receptive, of course, to other styles also. But when so much is anomalous about the landscape of learning, and when so many paradoxes and ironies mock the pretensions of founders and pioneers, it is reassuring to find some correspondences linking physical setting with human activity.

So far as monumentality and architectural decoration are concerned, this is a moment of reassessment. History has come, once again, to the rescue of revivalism, exposing the conceits supporting any effort to operate outside the need for adornment or temporal association. It is not clear how long this moment will last. But it provides the opportunity to reexamine the logic as well as the pieties of this older vocabulary. In the text that follows, Jean Block explores both with becoming fidelity, and restores to this campus the victory of intellectual intention it was meant to convey.

NEIL HARRIS

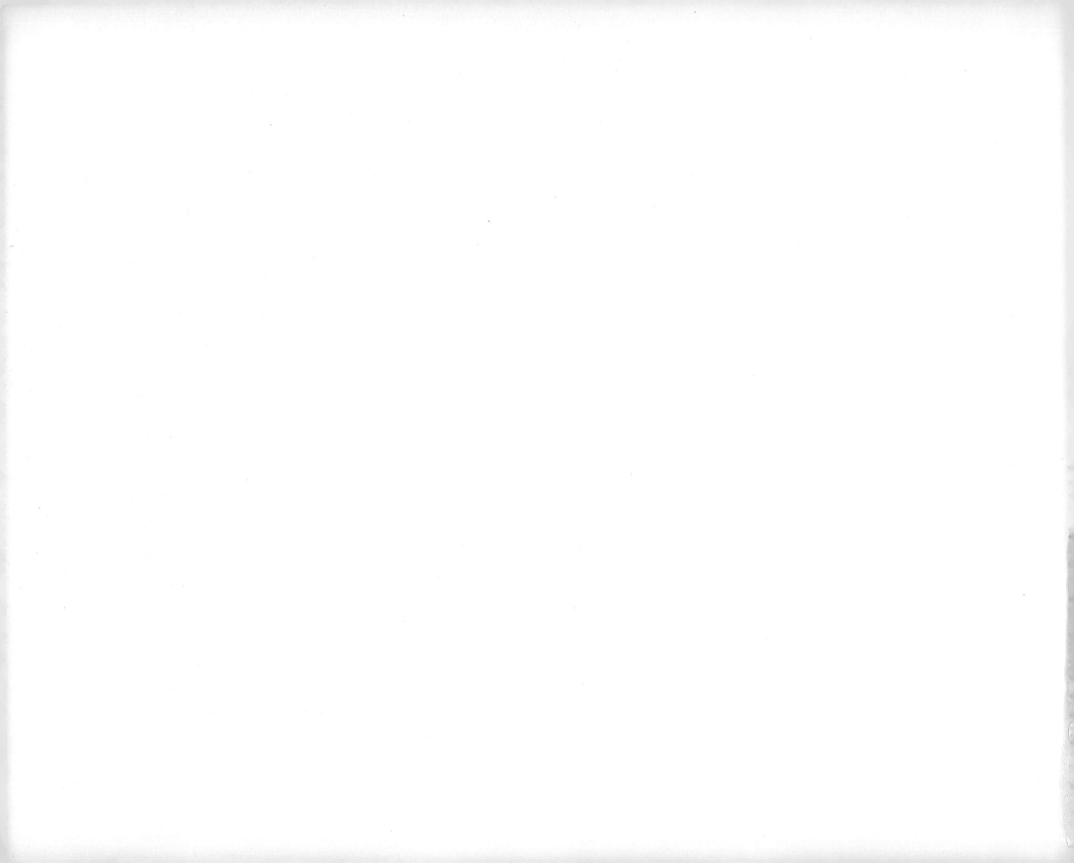

INTRODUCTION

Architecture stands in such an intimate relationship to man's physical and spiritual life that comment about it is frequently laden with moral phrases. Gothic architecture was, for the first forty years of the University of Chicago's existence, considered ennobling, inspiring, and uplifting. With the advent of a crusading modernism it was viewed as dishonest, deceptive, and irrelevant. We have only lately begun to take a less judgmental view. Now we can look at man's built environment with a detachment that enables us to see it in terms of its meaning to its creators and users and to place it in the context of its own time.

During the nineteenth century many institutions of higher education started with one or two buildings and added to them as need arose and donors appeared, often with chaotic results. When, in 1891, the new University of Chicago was faced with the challenge of building a campus, its trustees sought to assure an orderly development by beginning with a quadrangular plan and selecting an architectural style, Gothic, that would allow for variety within a unified whole. Gothic's venerability suited the idea of a long-range plan. If it could survive for five hundred years it could serve the University through its period of growth. Thus, while Gothic seemed to refer to the past, it was, in actuality, a commitment to the future.

From 1892 to 1932, the Gothic style and quadrangular plan governed a building program that provided a series of responses to the developing intellectual, social, and aesthetic needs of the University. Where the buildings were located, how they were planned, and the way they looked offer material evidence of this stage of the University's history. Secular Gothic, an inherently eclectic style, proved to be singularly flexible and readily subject to reinterpretation, reflecting the changes taking place within the University as well as in the wider community.

Building a campus is a communal work. The architect's clients—trustees and administrative officials—have clients of their own including donors, faculty, and students whose requirements must be met. Numerous and sometimes conflicting factors influence building decisions: availability of money, anticipated use, relationships with other buildings, and aesthetic appeal. As with any communal enterprise, the outcome is essentially centrist. The knowledge that buildings will be permanent tends to preclude risky innovation or experimentation. On the other hand, if the institution is not only to survive but to react to contemporary trends, it must go forward in its physical as well as its intellectual expression.

This exhibition and its catalogue are meant to show how the buildings of the period reflect the needs and aspirations of the University. The documents are drawn from the resources of the University of Chicago Archives: trustees and faculty minutes; correspondence of trustees, donors, faculty, administrators, and architects; building records; financial reports; and official University publications. They tell us who were making the decisions, how they were being made, for what reasons, and with what results. The archival photographs, maps, and plans give visual evidence of the ways in which the basic campus plan and architectural style evolved.

In order to keep the text for the exhibit as concise as possible, biographical and bibliographical information has been placed in the notes, as have some comments on matters that could only be touched upon in the exhibition. The notes are intended to help those who are interested in further research. Collections in the University Archives cited in the notes are in the Department of Special Collections, the Joseph Regenstein Library.

Many willing participants have aided this project. Special words of appreciation should go to Michael T. Ryan for his faith and encouragement at the outset; Robert R. Rosenthal, Jeffrey Abt, and Daniel Meyer for their careful scrutiny of the manuscript and many useful suggestions; Catharine Seybold, Linda Seidel, and Calvert W. Audrain for their helpful comments; and Cynthia Susmilch, who, with Jeffrey Abt, has designed this catalogue. Elizabeth Baltas assisted with typing the text and Susan

Kerr devoted many hours to making it comprehensible to the University's computer.

An exhibit of this kind is of necessity only a shimmer above the archival depths. If this one stimulates further inquiry, enriches understanding of the University's past, and contributes to an informed appreciation of its buildings, it will have fulfilled its purpose.

PART I

EMERGENCE OF A PLAN AND STYLE
1892-1900

THE GRAY CITY AND THE WHITE CITY

The Gray City of the University of Chicago and the White City of the World's Columbian Exposition were twin progeny of youthful Chicago, created by ardent, ambitious businessmen eager to change the city's image from one of barbarous materialism to one of refinement and culture.

There were striking parallels between the Gray City and the White City and equally striking differences. Both were located on adjacent plots of land in one of Chicago's newly annexed suburbs, Hyde Park, the University in an area between 57th and 59th Streets, the Exposition in Jackson Park and on the Midway Plaisance. Each was carefully planned before the first spadeful of earth was turned. They shared the competition for funds from Chicago's businessmen as well as competition for workmen and materials. [1] The architect selected by the University, Henry Ives Cobb, was on the National Board of Architects for the Exposition. [2] During the building period he was working on both sides of the Midway. A number of trustees of the new University were also directors of the Exposition. So close was the timing of their births that in December 1890, trustee Ferdinand Peck, who was vice-president of the Exposition, was forced to miss University President William Rainey Harper's Board of Trustees meeting because he was off to Washington to get President Harrison to issue the proclamation for the Exposition. [3]

The differences between the Exposition and the University were decisive, however, and so deeply felt by faculty and students that they were expressed repeatedly in subsequent years. The Exposition was seen as temporary, the University as eternal. The Exposition, particularly that part staged closest to the University, was intended to display, entertain, and astound. The University was dedicated to sober research and learning. While the Exposition plan was open and expansive, that of the University was cloistered and inward-looking. The Exposition

Site of the University of Chicago, 1891

Breaking ground on the Midway Plaisance for the World's Columbian Exposition, 1892. Courtesy of the Chicago Historical Society.

buildings were extravagantly ornate, as exemplified by Cobb's Fisheries Building. [4] Those of the University were, by comparison, austere. From the Ferris Wheel one could see Cobb's University buildings forming a dignified background for his exotic Streets of Algiers.

As William Gardner Hale, head professor of Latin, proclaimed at the July 1893 convocation, "another and more lasting vision has in these same years been silently rising under the shadow of the White City. When, by hard decree of necessity, the walls of that city have been razed to the ground, the Gray City of enduring stone by the Midway Plaisance will remain—witness to a still higher and more enduring idealism."[5]

So appealing was this distinction that it was incorporated the following year into the "Alma Mater":

> The City White hath fled the earth,
> But where the azure waters lie
> A nobler city hath its birth—
> The City Gray, that ne'er shall die!
> For decades and for centuries
> Its battlemented towers shall rise
> Beneath the hope-filled western skies. [6]

The Fisheries Building, World's Columbian Exposition, Henry Ives Cobb, 1893

View of the University of Chicago from the Ferris Wheel, 1893

The choice of Gothic for the University over the popular Classicism of the Exposition had its sources deep in the University's conception of itself. Classic buildings were financed by merchant princes, Gothic buildings arose through the combined efforts of humble workmen. Classicism referred to Europe's palaces, Gothic to Europe's great seats of learning. Classicism stood for the burgeoning materialism of the Renaissance, Gothic for timeless religious values.

The ecclesiastical metaphor was one which President Harper used easily. [7] "The university as priest, is a mediator between man and man; between man and man's own self; between mankind and that ideal inner self of mankind which merits and receives man's adoration . . . the university is the keeper, for the church of democracy, of holy mysteries, of sacred and significant traditions."[8]

CHAPTER 1

THE TRUSTEES' COMMITTEE ON BUILDINGS AND GROUNDS

Nine days after its charter was granted on July 1, 1890, the University's founders met and established the Trustees' Committee on Buildings and Grounds. Its task, implicit in its title but not spelled out, was to consider the site, prepare a plan, select an architect, and oversee the construction of the University's first buildings. The membership included Martin A. Ryerson, Charles L. Hutchinson, and Thomas W. Goodspeed, who served as secretary. [1]

Ryerson, who was to become president of the Board of Trustees, and Hutchinson, its treasurer, both in their middle thirties, served on this committee for the rest of their lives, providing, over a period of forty years, an organizational and aesthetic continuity that ensured the architectural unity of the

Martin A. Ryerson,
President of the Board of Trustees, 1892–1921

Thomas W. Goodspeed, Secretary of the Board of Trustees, 1891–1913

Charles L. Hutchinson,
Treasurer of the Board of Trustees, 1891–1925

William Rainey Harper,
President of the University, 1891–1906

9

Cobb's first drawings in the Romanesque style, May 30, 1891

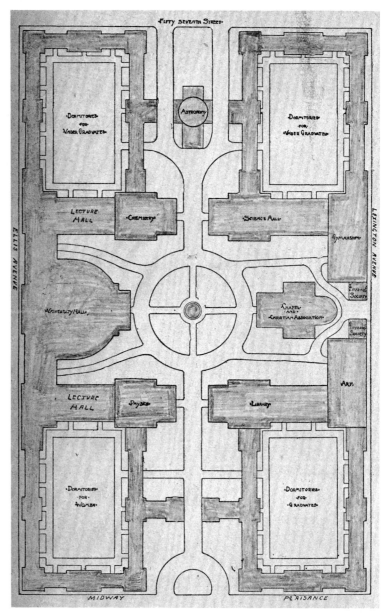

*Cobb's first plan, June 28, 1891, with buildings penciled in
by Trustee George C. Walker*

growing campus. Heirs to large fortunes, both maintained a strong sense of responsibility for the distribution of their wealth. Both were prominent in the development of Chicago's cultural institutions, and within the city's philanthropic elite each was acknowledged as a leader in the refinement of taste and style.

Ryerson in particular took an active part in the building plans for the University, discussing them with William Rainey Harper before the latter took up his presidency upon arriving from his professorship at Yale. Ryerson was also in close touch with Goodspeed, who, as the prime fund raiser for the Board of Trustees, was deeply involved in the physical planning.

Even before the first meeting of the Committee on Buildings and Grounds, Goodspeed was thinking in terms of a Gothic campus, urging Harper to visit Trinity College at Hartford, Connecticut,[2] and to obtain the plans of Yale's Gothic buildings.[3] Goodspeed envisioned quadrangles, but his own attempt to work this out on the three-block strip which Marshall Field had given the University shows how ill-adapted to this use the site would have been.[4]

The first problem the Committee on Buildings and Grounds addressed was that of the site. One block of the three-block strip was exchanged for an additional block on the Midway and another was purchased to expand the site to four square blocks, with the streets that separated them vacated. This meant that the campus could be designed in quadrangles rather than in a linear strip.[5]

The committee next voted to erect three buildings: a general recitation hall, a divinity school dormitory, and a graduate dormitory. It decided that five or six of the city's most eminent architects should be given its ideas and asked to submit plans.[6] Of the firms that were asked to submit sketches, Henry Ives Cobb, Patton and Fisher, and Flanders and Zimmerman responded. After some discussion and two votes, Cobb was chosen as architect for the first three buildings.[7]

The committee intensified its labors. During the summer of 1891 it met every four or five days, often with Cobb or one of his assistants, to make decisions that would lead to an orderly development of the building program. The first major decision had to do with architectural style. Cobb's drawings had

Perspective drawing of Cobb's second campus plan, 1892

University of Chicago
founded by
John D Rockefeller.

Henry Ives Cobb, Architect.

Perspective drawing of Cobb's final campus plan, 1893

12

been for buildings in the fashionable Romanesque idiom. [8] According to Goodspeed, Ryerson and Hutchinson undertook to persuade him to redesign them "in the very latest English Gothic."[9]

There were a number of practical reasons for the choice of Gothic in addition to the ideological reasons already mentioned. Paramount was the University's need to identify with the greatest European academic institutions, particularly those of England, which through their residential facilities fostered close relationships between scholars and students while providing a sense of protection that would be essential for an urban university. Gothic architecture was seen as providing adaptability and variety within a controlled plan. It was timeless. When money became available buildings could be added that would fit in with their predecessors.

The plan that finally evolved gave physical expression to the educational philosophy of the new University: quadrangles for graduates as well as undergraduates, women as well as men; spaces for a chapel, administration building, library, museums, and laboratories; small classrooms for in-dividualized teaching; and relatively few large lecture halls. [10]

But the plan had many flaws. It was too crowded. The chapel and administration building were far too large for the spaces allocated them. The uniform heights of the buildings and tightly closed quadrangles would have kept out the prevailing breezes. There was too little open space, and there were no axial vistas.

The first plan, and even the second[11] and third[12] were fantasies of an ideal university. They would undergo many changes. But the idea of a plan, the notion that the growth of the University would be stylistically consistent, contained, and articulated—safe from the whims and caprices of individual donors—would persist, promising, as Martin Ryerson said in his report to the trustees, "beauty, simplicity, and stability."

CHAPTER 2

A GENERAL RECITATION BUILDING

Henry Ives Cobb was a prominent institutional architect in a city noted for its commercial and residential buildings. Within ten years of his arrival in Chicago in 1881 he had received a number of important institutional commissions including the Chicago Opera House, Lake Forest College, and Northwestern University. His Venetian Gothic Athletic Club graced Michigan Avenue, and ground had recently been broken for his massive Romanesque Newberry Library. Negotiations were also underway for a new building for the Chicago Historical Society. [1]

Goodspeed, after talking to Cobb fully nine months before he was named architect for the University, sent Harper a sketch Cobb had made of a plan for a men's dormitory. [2] By the time the University

Henry Ives Cobb, University architect, 1891–1901

engaged him, Cobb had dissolved an earlier partnership with Charles Frost and was the sole leader of a bustling office, employing over a hundred men, designed to impress wealthy clients. [3]

Cobb Hall, the first building of the new University, was erected with money given by Silas B. Cobb. Not related to the architect, Silas Cobb was a pioneer Chicagoan who had arrived penniless in 1833 and over the years amassed a fortune. [4] The lecture hall proved to be Henry Ives Cobb's most expensive single building on the campus, [5] and, being the first, it was most influential in setting the architectural style for the subsequent forty years.

It was constructed of Blue Bedford limestone and roofed with copper-crested, flat red tiling. The trustees had at first feared that they could not afford limestone and would have to make do with brick, and later that not enough Bedford limestone would be available to go forward with the contract. The contractor was successful, however, in locating a source, and the decision was made to use Bedford limestone. This decision proved to be a crucial one, for, in the interest of preserving an appearance of unity, limestone became the predominant building material for the University. [6]

Cobb Hall from the east, Henry Ives Cobb, 1892

John D. Rockefeller, Founder of the University,
portrait by Eastman Johnson, 1894

Using a few well-selected elements of the Gothic vocabulary—steep-roofed gables, turrets, and dormers, topped by occasional crockets and finials, deep-set rectangular windows, five-sided oriels at the corners of the jutting pavilions, and slender towers flanking the main entrance—Cobb created a variegated surface that was constantly responsive to changes in lighting and produced a dramatic silhouette that broke the flat and spare terrain. He added judiciously chosen ornamentation, particularly around the main entrance with its bossed pointed arch, carved spandrels, and rising tiers of traceried windows.

Inside, Cobb Hall was starkly functional. The walls were faced with brick and in general were bare except for the portrait of the Founder, John D. Rockefeller, which hung in the chapel in the building's north end. Planning for the allocation of space had been going on for over a year, keyed to the unfolding of Harper's educational scheme. The first floor housed the chapel, a large lecture hall, offices for the University Extension, the University Press, and ample space for the deans who would provide close faculty-student contacts. Initially, the President's office was in the southeast corner of this

Cobb Hall lecture room

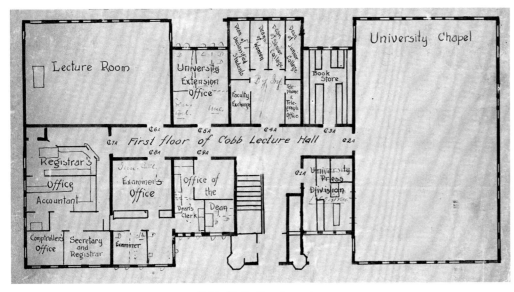

Cobb Hall, first floor plan

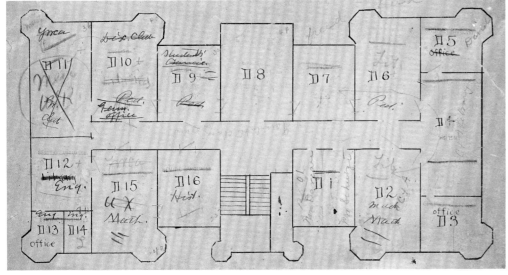

Cobb Hall, fourth floor plan, showing changes in room use

floor. The second, third, and fourth floors were devoted to individual departments, each with its offices, classrooms, and a library. The assignment of these rooms was not meant to be permanent as departments rotated in and out of them as space became available elsewhere.

The trustees' intimate involvement was evident in the last-minute preparations for the opening of the University: President Harper presented a list of the furniture needed and Goodspeed was instructed to obtain bids; Ryerson was authorized to secure an electric clock and also to provide hooks for students' hats and coats. [7]

Marked only by a simple chapel service, the opening of the University on October 1, 1892, was widely covered by the Chicago press. The plan in general and the completed buildings—Cobb Hall, and the divinity and graduate dormitories—were described as massive, imposing, majestic, and monumental, providing a "vast facade, uniform in material and color, but so varied as to relieve any monotony of outline."[8]

CHAPTER 3

A HOUSING SYSTEM FOR MEN

The arrangement of the residential quadrangles into sections for divinity students, graduate men, undergraduate men, and women was intended to provide a congenial intellectual and social life on campus. Thomas Goodspeed, himself a minister, had some apprehensions about the housing for the seminary students. "When they are in any way kept separate," he wrote Harper, "the College men are disposed to regard them as a little—what shall I say? My view was that if put into the same buildings they would do the College men good. There would be more fellow feeling. There would be more openness of life in the University. A more sturdy, manly, muscular Christianity in the Div. School; a more quiet, refined and less boisterous animal life in the college."[1] Harper did not agree. "On the whole, I am afraid it would spoil

Cobb Hall and the men's residences from the west, Henry Ives Cobb, 1892

Snell Hall, Henry Ives Cobb, 1893

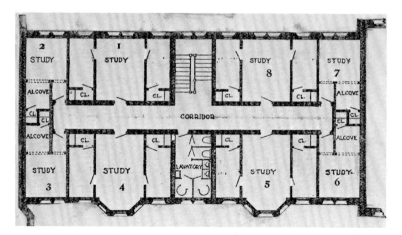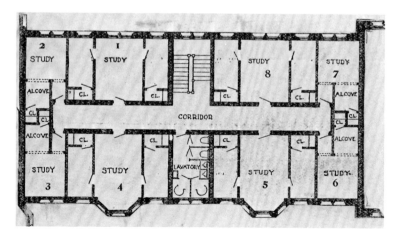

Graduate dormitory (now Blake Hall) floor plans

the spirit of the theological students as well as of the others to have them mingled."[2]

The matter was quickly settled when John D. Rockefeller contributed $100,000 for divinity dormitories, later named Gates Hall and Goodspeed Hall. These, together with the graduate dormitory, later named Blake Hall, erected alongside Cobb Hall, formed the first of the University's campus facades. Henry Ives Cobb was able to achieve both continuity and variety by recalling the oriels of Cobb Hall in the bays of the dormitories and by making Gates Hall five instead of four stories high.

Snell Hall for undergraduate men, given by Mrs. Henrietta Snell in memory of her husband, A. J. Snell, was completed a year later in 1893. With its projecting bay, crocketed gables, and ornamented entrance, it was very similar to the other dormitories.

Each dormitory housed fifty men, most in suites consisting of a study and two small bedrooms. Furnishings were provided by Charles Hutchinson and other trustees and donors. The furnishings were minimal, but the comfort of the divinity students was soon enhanced by "certain sympathetic sewing

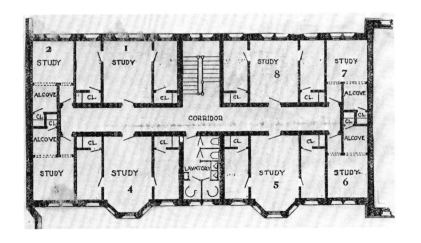
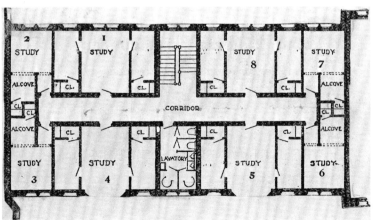

Oct 1894

Snell 1895

Chicago Oct 26

Mr R W Harper

Dear Sir

your letter was received this Morning. I send you 200.00 by my Maid it will help to get things for the Snell Hall I am wishing for Better times I remain

Yours Sincerely

Mrs Henrietta Snell

Henrietta Snell to President Harper, October 26, 1894

Feb. 15, 1894

Rev. T. W. Goodspeed,
Secretary of the Board of Trustees.

Dear Sir,—

That the accompanying petition to the Board of Trustees may not seem to you a hasty or inconsiderate measure, we would have you know that after hearing the individual sentiments of its members toward the resolution, the House appointed a committee to investigate the matter of rents in the vicinity of the University. This committee found that within almost a stone's throw of the campus furnished rooms, steam-heated and furnished with gas and baths can be procured for one dollar and a quarter per week: also that within four blocks, rooms elegantly furnished and having most attractive outlooks, provided with call-bells by which servants may be summoned, supplied with baths, and accessible by elevator, can be procured for two dollars per week. In consideration of this report of its committee the House decided to include in its resolution the clause suggesting that the reduction be upon a scale of twenty-five per cent., which suggestion, in view of the facts, seemed modest.

The above is wholly inofficial, though it can readily be substantiated if desired. I mention the facts at the suggestion of our House Counselor, thinking they may have some explanatory value to yourself and the gentlemen of the Board of Trustees.

I remain, Very respectfully,

Paul F. Carpenter,
Secy. Snell House.

societies" who supplied them with embroidered foot-rests and sofa pillows. [3]

There were, at first, no provisions for the group life that was felt to be so desirable. Commenting on some early problems, the *University of Chicago Weekly* reported, "In constructing Snell Hall the University authorities did their best to defeat the very object for which they were ostensibly striving—that of making social life a regular part of the college life. They provided absolutely no place for the assembling of residents of the hall. The need of such a place was so evident from the first that a fine club room was soon fitted up in the basement and one of the rooms on the first floor was turned into a parlor. Mrs. Snell, the donor of the hall, has done much to make it more suitable."[4] Mrs. Snell did indeed rally with a piano, a check, and "best wishes for the boys' rapid progress in their studies."[5]

At the beginning of its second year, in an attempt to provide a working structure, the University adopted a house system. Each house had a head appointed by President Harper, a counselor chosen from the faculty by house members, and a secretary and treasurer elected by house members. Membership was determined by those already in the house, "assuring congeniality."[6]

With the onset of the depression of 1893, dormitory building was postponed, and apartments and fraternities were operated as part of the University's housing. More than 40 percent of the students took advantage of the plethora of neighborhood rooming houses and hotels that had been built for the Exposition. A committee of students petitioned the trustees for a decrease in housing fees, arguing that it was cheaper and more comfortable—indeed luxurious—to live outside the housing system. [7]

President Harper's ideal of a collegial setting was far from fulfillment.

CHAPTER 4

A RESIDENTIAL PROGRAM FOR WOMEN

If the purpose of the house system for men was to provide collegiality and comradeship, for women, according to Dean Marion Talbot, it aimed to "enrich the nature and develop the character . . . as well as correlate the discipline of the classroom with the demands of life."[1]

President Harper, hoping to create an environment that would be attractive, safe, and well-controlled, appointed three deans of women among the first officers of his administration: Alice Freeman Palmer, Marion Talbot, and Julia Bulkley. Mrs. Palmer and Miss Talbot assumed responsibility for the living arrangements, social life, and general well-being of the young women of the University.[2]

As a former president of Wellesley College Mrs.

Alice Freeman Palmer, Professor of History and Dean of Women, 1892–95

Palmer was thoroughly acquainted with the problems and challenges of women's residences. Miss Talbot, also from Wellesley, joined the faculty as an assistant professor of sanitary science in the Department of Sociology.[3] As founders of the Association of Collegiate Alumnae, they were dedicated advocates of educational opportunities for women. Both were interested in bringing scientific rigor to what were regarded as women's traditional roles in the family and home.[4]

Because designs for the first women's dormitories were still incomplete when the University opened, Mrs. Palmer and Miss Talbot were able to influence the planning. During the first year, women and some faculty were housed in the Beatrice, a nearby apartment building. Marion Talbot wrote to her parents that immediately upon arriving at the Beatrice, "Mrs. Palmer and I went at the President's request, to see Mr. Henry Ives Cobb . . . and inspect the plans of the women's dormitories. We found some woeful mistakes, such as no rooms *en suite*, no fireplaces, no parlor for the household, no provision for ventilation."[5] But the plans they saw had already been revised from Cobb's first proposal, which would have been far too costly to attract a

Marion Talbot, Assistant Professor of Sanitary Science, Professor of Household Management, and Dean of Women, 1892–1925

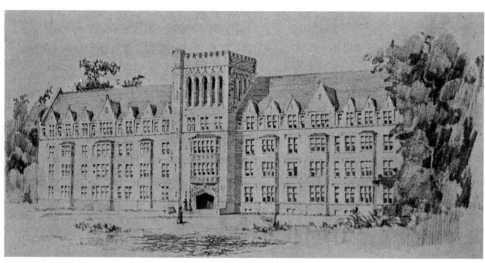

Cobb's sketch for a women's dormitory, The Graphic, *April 23, 1892*

donor.[6] Essentially it was the same plan as that for the men's dormitories: units of two bedrooms and a study placed along either side of a long central corridor. Cobb had added a romantic tower that would provide a large "play room or assembly room" and a roof where the young women could "sit in pleasant weather overlooking the College grounds."[7]

By May, this proposed single building had been broken down into several smaller ones, each esti-

PLANS SUGGESTED FOR BUILDINGS FOR WOMEN.

Drawings presented in Appeal on Behalf of Women Students *by the Women's Club of Chicago, 1892*

mated at $50,000, which were depicted in a brochure prepared for potential donors.[8] Following their meeting with Cobb, Mrs. Palmer appealed to the Trustees' Committee on Buildings and Grounds, and the Cobb plans were modified again.[9]

These first women's residences were the gifts of Mrs. Nancy Foster, Mrs. Jerome Beecher, and Mrs. Hiram Kelly, who was the donor of both Kelly and Green Halls.[10] The plans indicate, in addition to the parlors and dining rooms to assure sociability and hospitality, a regard for the need for independence and privacy in individual rooms. Instead of the two-bedroom and study units most of the rooms are single with connecting doors allowing the creation of suites.

The exteriors reflected the Gothic ambiance of the men's dormitories to the west: Bedford limestone, red-tiled roofs with copper crestings and finials, arched and ornamented doorways, foils and cusps in a few high windows, and oriels and bays. When all the buildings were completed they formed the eastern facade of the quadrangles as the men's buildings formed that on the west. Like Gates Hall, its counterpart across the campus, Green Hall was

A student room in Green Hall, 1900

Women's residences from the northwest

made five stories high thus adding variety to the roof line. In deference to its position on the Midway, facing the Exposition, the southeast turrets of Foster Hall presented a veritable forest of crockets and bands of gargoyles peering over the unpaved street below.[11] The west wall of Foster Hall was blank brick in anticipation of the addition completed in 1901. Kelly and Beecher Halls, mirror images of each other, were separated by the foundation for Green Hall, not to be finished until 1898.

The women's residences became centers for campus parties and receptions. In the men's dormitories it was joked that being a resident head quickly drove a man into matrimony. In the women's dormitories, however, the resident heads—Marion Talbot, Sophonisba Breckinridge, Elizabeth Wallace, and Myra Reynolds—tended to settle in and make homes for themselves. Marion Talbot lived in Green Hall from 1896 until her retirement in 1925.

The women's dormitories succeeded in a way that the first men's did not by providing an appealing, well-managed life for their residents. By 1902, Snell Hall had been turned over for the use of the YMCA. The women's halls, on the other hand, evoked loyalty and affection. Professor James Westfall

Marion Talbot's room in Green Hall

Thompson shrugged off the difference, saying, "The essential reason for the variation apparent between the social life of the men and of the women seems to be the fact that the women enjoy real home life, while the men do not."[12] A more likely explanation would appear to be that the women deans, sensitive to how much the academic success of the students rode on good living arrangements, invested more effort in physical planning and devoted more time to articulating and developing a social purpose for women's residences.

Foster Hall interior

Foster Hall from the Midway, 1893

CHAPTER 5

MUSEUMS AND PEDAGOGY

As the building program proceeded, the geometry of the plan was maintained, along with a consistency in building materials and use of Gothic motifs, but the functions of the buildings were altered, particularly as the pressure for teaching space increased. An advantage inherent in the choice of the Gothic style was that it allowed for this kind of modification in individual buildings while providing a sense of stability and harmony for the overall campus plan.

Walker Museum, dedicated in December 1893, occupied the north end of the women's quadrangle, a space initially allocated to the general library. George C. Walker intended it to be a great museum of natural history. [1] Planning for the museum was chiefly the work of Walker and Cobb in consultation with Thomas Chrowder Chamberlin, president of the University of Wisconsin, who was to head both the museum and the Department of Geology at Chicago. [2]

The museum was Cobb's first campus building to face two quadrangles. To conserve wall space for the exhibits, the staircase tower was placed on the south. [3] Space was thus freed for an immense exhibit hall high enough to house an anticipated collection of large prehistoric skeletons. [4] The entrance to the exhibit hall was through the great north doorway, which, like Cobb's other entrances, was arched and ornamented, surmounted by tiers of cusped windows.

But even as the museum was going up, the pressure for classroom space was so intense and the constraints on building imposed by the depression of 1893 so severe that it was decided to locate the geology department on the second floor. Chamberlin worked out a plan for dividing the space into classrooms, laboratories, library, and lecture hall. [5] But the plan approved by the trustees involved only three walls and used exhibit cases for partitions, an expression of faith that in time the space would revert to its original purpose. [6]

Staircase tower of Walker Museum, Henry Ives Cobb, 1893

At the opening, Harper rejoiced that "the building for a museum has come to us before a library building," because the city was full of valuable collections about to be distributed. [7] He was, of course, referring to the exhibits at the Exposition. Many of these, however, either returned to their country of origin or went to the Field Columbian Museum of Natural History when it opened in the Exposition's Fine Arts Building in Jackson Park in 1895.

Chamberlin and the Committee on Museums determined that the museums should serve the University's study and research purposes rather than the public, and that there should be a general museum center and departmentalized units. [8] A plan for a general museum never materialized. When the biological laboratories were built, the appropriate collections were sent there, while Walker Museum became primarily a paleontology collection. Reciprocal arrangements were worked out with the Field Museum, and in time even the paleontology materials went there. Meanwhile the ever-growing geology and geography departments continued to fill the space. Twenty-two years would pass before they would have their own quarters.

Walker Museum exhibit hall, 1898

Mrs. Frederick Haskell was inspired by her pastor, the Reverend John Henry Barrows, to establish a museum devoted to the study of the Oriental roots of the Jewish and Christian religions. [9] Gothic notes of permanence and immortality were struck at the laying of the cornerstone of Haskell Oriental Museum in 1895 when Harper spoke of the building which "shall stand possibly for five centuries," [10] and Barrows praised the donors of the University and its beautiful architecture and predicted that a century hence the Haskell Oriental Museum would be surrounded by groups of academic buildings that

Walker Museum, north entrance

Cornerstone ceremonies for Haskell Oriental Museum, 1894

would "repeat many of the glories so dear to Oxford."[11]

Like Walker Museum, Haskell Oriental Museum was slipped into a slot designated in the plan for another use, dormitories. Also, like Walker Museum, its expanse of space invited an influx of students and faculty, this time from the Divinity School. Haskell Museum's skylighted third floor exhibit space was taken over by the Divinity School library. Gradually the Divinity School took over other parts of the building as well.

Again, like Walker Museum, Haskell Oriental Museum fronted on two quadrangles. Cobb felt it "unnecessary to make the building at all ornate in its outline. . . . the most important part of the building will in the future be the close view of the main entrance, which I have endeavored to make attractive."[12] The west entrance, facing the austere men's dormitories—Gates, Blake, and Goodspeed—is simple to the point of severity. The east entrance is marked by an elaborate doorway, above which rises a gable punctured with a traceried window. The whole building is designed to admit a maximum of light with broad bands of windows between the

Divinity School library in Haskell Oriental Museum

East front of Haskell Oriental Museum, Henry Ives Cobb, 1896

buttresses and has, instead of Cobb's usual arrangement of dormers and gables, a peaked sky-lighted roof.

Professor James Henry Breasted was most active in assembling the museum's collections. The museum was, from the outset, seen as a teaching medium. [13] Unlike Walker Museum, however, Haskell Oriental Museum drew support from a public constituency, first the Egyptian Exploration Fund and later, in response to a proffer of $50,000 from John D. Rockefeller, the Oriental Exploration Fund, set up under the auspices of the University. [14] This meant that there would be an audience outside of the University and an obligation to present exhibits for it. Despite its space problems, Haskell Oriental Museum survived, its collections constantly growing.

Providing spaces for research and teaching remained a pressing problem for the University at the end of the nineteenth century. The surge of students and professors into the museum spaces was contrary to the expectations of donors, trustees, and architect and radically altered the use for which these buildings had been intended.

Haskell Oriental Museum interiors, 1898

CHAPTER 6

LABORATORIES FOR THE SCIENCES

Within five years of the University's opening, all of the sciences, with the exception of geology, were housed in their own buildings, indicating the University's strong commitment to basic scientific research. [1] Kent Chemical Laboratory[2] and Ryerson Physical Laboratory opened January 1, 1894. [3] The Hull Biological Laboratories—Physiology, Zoology, Anatomy, and Botany[4]—and Yerkes Observatory were completed in 1897. [5]

The Chemical Laboratory, given by Sidney A. Kent,[6] and the Physical Laboratory donated by Martin A. Ryerson, [7] rose in Gothic grandeur on either side of the north-south roadway that traversed the main quadrangle. Structurally similar, they are rectangular buildings with crocketed gables topping jut-

Kent Chemical Laboratory, Henry Ives Cobb, 1894

Ryerson Physical Laboratory, Henry Ives Cobb, 1894

ting pavilions at either end, peaked dormers projecting from steep roofs, and center portions marked by ornate entrances and towers. The effect of the design is essentially the same as that of Cobb Hall. The use of projections and voids is most striking on Ryerson Physical Laboratory with its balconies, recessed arcade over the entrance, window slits in the tower, and lancet windows in the dormers and gables. From the molding beneath the parapet project the heads of gargoyles. Ryerson Physical Laboratory was acclaimed by President Harper as the most beautiful university building in the world.[8] The rear, or north side of Ryerson, before its annex was later attached, is identical in

Aerial view of the University from the Midway showing north-south tree-lined driveway, 1896

Ryerson Physical Laboratory from the north, ca. 1900

outline to the south facade, except for the lack of entrance, balconies, and tower, and paucity of window tracery. It was obviously the back.

Kent was distinguished by its crocketed conical turret and elaborate wrought iron doorstraps. On the north side of Kent is a large circular hall, resembling a chapter house, which served as a lecture hall and chapel.

The interiors of these two laboratories were planned with the greatest attention to the functional requirements of research. Ira Remsen, the eminent chemist at Johns Hopkins University, was a consultant on the design and equipment of Kent, and the University's head professor of physics, Albert A. Michelson, was adviser for Ryerson Laboratory.[9]

Extraordinary construction problems posed by the science buildings—foundations and walls that would minimize external vibrations; highly specialized spaces including constant temperature rooms, iron-free laboratories, dark rooms, and gas analysis

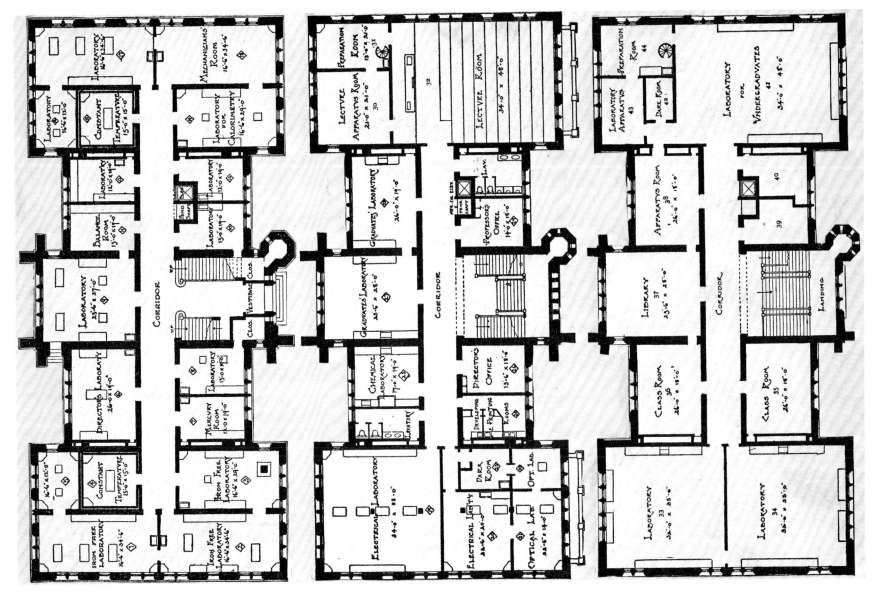

Ryerson Laboratory floor plan

Botany Building, Henry Ives Cobb, 1897

rooms—all contributed to the buildings' high cost. As a result of their experience with Ryerson Physical Laboratory and Kent Chemical Laboratory, both of which had far exceeded expected costs, the trustees urged Cobb to simplify the treatment of the biological laboratories and allow for as much light and space as possible. [10]

The four biology buildings, gift of Miss Helen Culver, [11] were plain, rectangular in shape, and connected by low cloisters to form three sides of a quadrangle. Evenly spaced double-hung windows marked the first three floors. Above them, slender columns divided the dormer windows. As in other Cobb buildings, visual interest was centered on the

Physiology Building, Henry Ives Cobb, 1897

Anatomy Building and Cobb Gate, Henry Ives Cobb, 1897

main entrance. An occasional griffin topped a steep gable. Always conscious of the effect of the entrance, Cobb judiciously placed the tall third floor anatomical theater next to the approach to the quadrangle from 57th Street, providing a dramatic note which is heightened by the imposing gate with its clambering grotesques. The gate was a gift from the architect, designed with a Gothic flourish that economic strictures had often prevented him from using elsewhere on campus.

The contrast between the ebullient symbolism of the Cobb gate and the gaunt simplicity of the Hull Biological Laboratories reflected the tension between the trappings of medievalism and the demands of modern science. While Gothic architecture nourished the University's sense of its identity, some felt that medievalism should not permeate campus life. The adoption of medieval ceremonies and garb for convocations, for instance, did not go uncriticized. Thomas Chrowder Chamberlin thought them monastic and protested the revival of "the ceremonials of medieval institutions which . . . are associated with an undeveloped stage of scholarship. . . . real scholarship . . . associates itself more and more with simplicity."[12] Dean Harry Pratt Judson also found that "all this

frippery of colors and tinsel is a distinct retrogression to the customs of the dark ages."[13]

The conflict was rationalized in the sonnet written about Cobb Gate by Howard Spencer Fiske, in which the medieval grotesques of the entrance are associated with superstition and fear, and the campus beyond with freedom and "the courts of truth."

> No porter's lodge along the Oxford High
>   On proctor-shadowed student from his rouse
>   So grimly frowned as thou; nor blackened boughs
> On Dante losing, hopeless, earth and sky.
> Thy crocket crawlers scare the helpless eye;
>   Thine anguished corbels twist their human brows;
>   Thy dragon kneelers bend to wicked vows;
> And high-perched finials threat the passer-by.
> And yet through such as thou the race has passed
>   To freedom—superstition's dreadful gate
>   Hath oped upon the courts of truth at last;
> Nor all the fears of an imagined fate,
>   Nor all the goblin crew of error vast
>   Can shut the mind from learning's fair estate.[14]

CHAPTER 7

THE END OF THE COBB YEARS

By 1900, Cobb's relationship with the University was drawing to a close. There had been a growing discontent with Cobb and the way his office operated. As early as 1891 Goodspeed complained, "We have found it simply impossible to hurry Mr. Cobb. We have haunted his office. We have multiplied meetings of the B'l'd'g Committee. We have urged, exhorted, entreated, in short we have exhausted all the resources of pressure on him in vain. It has been impossible to hasten his pace by the fractional part of a second."[1] In 1892, the Trustees' Committee on Buildings and Grounds instructed Goodspeed to notify Cobb that the committee was disappointed with his plans, and that unless the work of the University could receive more attention and go forward more rapidly the committee would feel compelled to ask for the as-

The University of Chicago.

W. R. HARPER, PRESIDENT OF UNIVERSITY.
E. NELSON BLAKE, PRESIDENT OF BOARD.

C. L. HUTCHINSON, TREASURER.
T. W. GOODSPEED, SECRETARY.

Office: 1212 CHAMBER OF COMMERCE.

Chicago, _Oct. 12_ _1891_

Goodspeed to Harper, October 12, 1891

sistance of another architect.[2] There were faculty complaints as well. William Gardner Hale, a member of the Faculty Committee on Buildings and Grounds, wrote to Hutchinson protesting that Cobb's interiors were cheerless and gloomy and that he could not think well of an architect who, in one building after another, tolerated such poor work.[3] Helen Culver queried the lack of supervision during the building of the Hull Laboratories and wondered about the "moral responsibility of the architect."[4]

Cobb clearly understood the importance of his work for the University. "I realize that so far as the buildings are concerned," he wrote Goodspeed, "I have more at stake in that University than any one else connected with it."[5]

Cobb was encouraged to think in monumental terms, particularly by President Harper, but his designs often proved too grandiose either to attract a donor or to fit into the campus plan. The scale of Cobb's proposed chapel was too large for the central quadrangle, and the gymnasium which would have occupied a complete city block was entirely beyond the University's meager resources.

Cobb's study for a University chapel

When Cobb opened a Washington office in 1900 to pursue a national practice, the trustees began to doubt that the University was receiving his full attention. Although Cobb insisted in a letter to Harper that he was still very much interested in the University,[6] the Trustees' Committee on Buildings and Grounds recommended in 1901 that the relationship be terminated.[7]

Cobb's legacy to the University was substantial and lasting. Though far from completion, his plan for an enclosed campus community would continue to shape future building projects. The buildings themselves were Cobb's dignified and durable interpretations of a historical style, bringing a sense of tradition and permanence to the featureless prairie landscape. By creating an ensemble of buildings related to each other in their common use of Gothic but varied in their treatment of individual details, Cobb opened the way for similar personal expressions of the style by his successors.

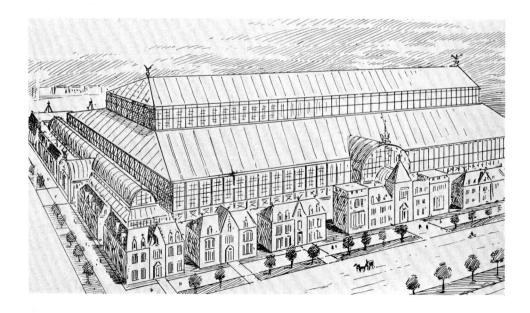

Cobb's drawing for a gymnasium and covered athletic field

EASTERN OFFICE.
1759 N STREET,
WASHINGTON, D.C.

GOVERNMENT OFFICE.
TREASURY, DEPARTMENT.
WASHINGTON, D.C.

WESTERN OFFICE.
100 WASHINGTON STREET,
CHICAGO, ILLINOIS.

PERSONAL.

HENRY IVES COBB
ARCHITECT.

Washington, D.C., January 23, 1900.

Dr. William R. Harper,

University of Chicago,

Chicago, Ill.

Dear Doctor:-

From something you said when we met in New York
the other day and from information I get from Chicago, I fear that
the stories of my having left Chicago being so diligently circulated
by people more interested in my abuse than my welfare, have made some
impression on you and the Trustees of the University of Chicago.
In point of fact my office in Chicago has not been as active in years
as it is at the present moment; nor has my organization there
been as good; and although my practice is extending more and more
over the country I still keep in close touch with my Chicago office,
and run the constructional side of all my Western work from that
office. I am constantly in Chicago, but I devote my entire attention wherever I am to my work, and when in Chicago, or any other
City, I am absorbed in it.

I have not left Chicago nor have I any intention of doing
so, but am striving to the best of my ability for something more
than simply local reputation and practice, and with much greater
success than I expected when I first determined to make the attempt,
as after three years I have a number of very important and interesting buildings in different parts of the country. I fully apprec-

Cobb to Harper, January 23, 1900

Building entrances designed by Cobb

PART II

ASSIMILATION OF GOTHIC FORMS
1901-1916

CHAPTER 8

OXFORD COMES TO CHICAGO

T he University's Decennial Celebration, held in June 1901, was a time for looking backward with pride and forward with optimism. In the preceding decade nineteen permanent buildings had been erected. By the twenty-fifth anniversary sixteen more would be added, plans completed for the central quadrangles, and the entire campus, sorely ravaged by excavations and earth-moving, landscaped.

Several changes, both in external circumstances and in perceptions of the University's needs, had occurred since the early nineties. The depression had lifted, and the efforts of Harper and the trustees to find donors were succeeding. Furthermore, John D. Rockefeller was now persuaded to contribute not only for endowment but for building as well. [1]

DAYS WITH PEOPLE—MR. ROCKEFELLER.

Harper's fund-raising caricatured, Chicago Daily News, *February 1900*

As the financial situation eased there was a shift in building priorities. In the pressure to establish the University as a research institution, amenities for students had perforce been given second place, but these needs could no longer be ignored. Throughout the United States enrollments in higher education had been increasing rapidly, rising from 70,000 students in 1870 to 233,000 in 1900. [2] The University had always believed in the importance of a collegial atmosphere, but there was now a sense that if it were to attract the best students it would have to provide a pleasant environment. This was particularly true in the case of men students, for by 1900 the number of women was beginning to exceed that of men. Dormitory, eating, and recreational facilities for men assumed prime importance. [3]

A second urgent necessity was spaces for large groups; the student body had increased from 594 in 1892 to 2,431 in 1901, [4] and the largest hall on campus, Kent lecture hall, could seat only 500. Buildings for the professional schools, humanities, social sciences, geology, geography, and for a library were yet to be provided.

These needs were spelled out repeatedly by Presi-

dent Harper. As the money became available, the new campus architects, Shepley, Rutan and Coolidge, principally, but also Dwight Heald Perkins, James Gamble Rogers, and Holabird and Roche, brought their own individual interpretations to the problems of adapting the Gothic style to the University's needs.

When the University celebrated its Decennial, presentation drawings and plans had been completed for Mitchell Tower, Mandel Hall, Hutchinson Commons, the Reynolds Club, and Hitchcock Hall. The President, the Founder, trustees, faculty, donors, and friends of donors trooped from cornerstone to cornerstone, and all of the speeches underscored the initial goals of an identification with Oxford: tradition, collegiality, beauty, and immortality, goals that would stabilize, solidify, and perpetuate the raw young University.

For conservative and radical alike, the alliance with Oxonian traditionalism validated the University. At the cornerstone-laying for Hutchinson Commons, Albion Small, professor in the new Department of Sociology, said, "For the first time we turn to a definite time and place in the old world for support

Drawing for the Tower Group, Shepley, Rutan and Coolidge, 1901

Drawing for Hitchcock Hall, Dwight Heald Perkins, 1901

and enrichment of our modern enterprise. It is both a mark and a means of personal and social growth to be able, without self-reproach, to acknowledge dependence on the past."

Professor George E. Vincent emphasized the importance of buildings dedicated to the art of living. "The University takes pride in her laboratories, but she also covets for her students something of the charm of life in the cloisters of Oxford and Cambridge."

Mitchell Tower was seen as coordinating all the other buildings into one harmonious whole. It signaled a new prosperity which permitted erecting a building with no utilitarian value, whose sole purpose was to add beauty to the campus.

Professor Paul Shorey invoked the timelessness of Oxford to suggest the immortality of the donor. "Mrs. Hitchcock has walked in the closes of Oxford and beside the chapels of Cambridge and has admired the foundations that bear the names of mediaeval queens and noble ladies. And the thought that in the days that shall call this morning ancient, she shall be numbered of a like company may well bring the flush to her brow and the throb to her heart."[5]

Cornerstone ceremonies for Hitchcock Hall, 1901, showing Mrs. Charles Hitchcock, Dean Harry Pratt Judson, and Dwight Heald Perkins

Cornerstone ceremonies for the Tower Group, 1901

CHAPTER 9

THE TOWER GROUP

At the turn of the century Martin Ryerson and Charles Hutchinson were influential in engaging Charles Coolidge of the Boston firm of Shepley, Rutan and Coolidge, and in redefining the Gothic idiom. [1]

Hutchinson, as president of the Art Institute, and Ryerson, as a member of its building committee, had worked with Coolidge when he was designing the new museum erected in conjunction with the World's Columbian Exposition. [2] Concurrently the firm won a competition for the Chicago Public Library, thus establishing itself, with Cobb, as preeminent among the designers of institutional architecture in Chicago. [3]

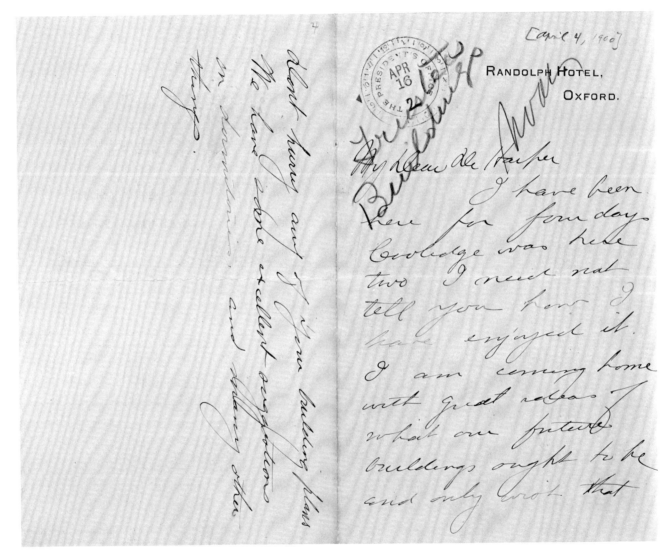

[April 4, 1900]

RANDOLPH HOTEL,
OXFORD.

My Dear Dr Harper

I have been
here for four days
Coolidge was here
two I need not
tell you how I
have enjoyed it.
I am coming home
with great ideas of
what our future
buildings ought to be
and only wish that

Bushnell H

you were here and I your building plans
We have some excellent suggestions
in Somewhere and altering after
things.

Charles Hutchinson to President Harper, April 4, 1900

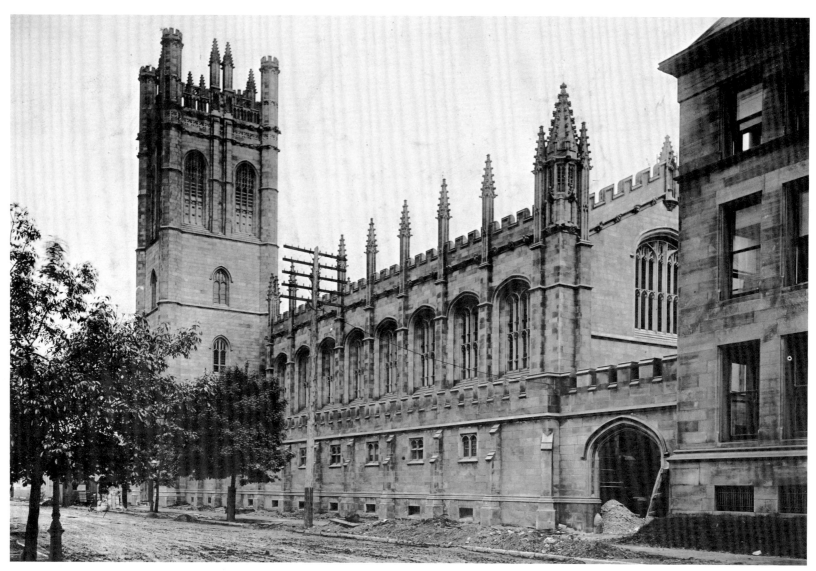

Hutchinson Commons and Mitchell Tower from the northwest, Shepley, Rutan and Coolidge, 1903

Shepley, Rutan and Coolidge had been co-draftsmen in the offices of Henry Hobson Richardson and, after his death in 1886, had formed their own firm. In 1888, they prepared the master plan for Stanford University, like the University of Chicago a pioneer in campus planning. When work started on the Art Institute and the Chicago Public Library, the firm opened an office in Chicago and arranged to have Coolidge in residence. Close personal friendships developed between the Coolidges and the Ryersons and Hutchinsons. [4] The Art Institute experience was apparently an exemplary architect-client relationship, and its trustees recorded their complete satisfaction with Coolidge's taste, skill, and unflagging attention. [5]

In April 1900, Hutchinson and Coolidge visited Oxford together with a view to making plans for a refectory (which would be the gift of Hutchinson), men's club, auditorium, and bell tower. From Oxford, Hutchinson wrote President Harper, "I am coming home with great ideas of what our future buildings ought to be and only wish that we might begin all over again. . . . I have men working in Christ Church Hall taking measurements." [6]

In June, the Trustees' Committee on Buildings and Grounds recommended to the Board of Trustees that Shepley, Rutan and Coolidge be made architects for the commons, club house, and assembly hall, and the recommendation was approved. [7]

The Tower Group, completed in 1903, was designed to meet the need for student amenities and group spaces. The University took pride in the knowledge that these buildings were derived from specific Oxford structures: Hutchinson Commons from Christ Church Hall, the Reynolds Club from St. John's College, and Mitchell Tower from the bell-tower of Magdalen College. [8]

They are not, however, slavish copies. [9] Coolidge selected, altered, and recombined the Oxonian forms with imagination, flexibility, and responsiveness to the demands of the University. Adapting Christ Church Hall for use as a men's commons, Coolidge added broad parapeted side aisles, on the north to provide a food preparation and service area, and on the south to furnish space for a cafe. In the design of the tower, too, Coolidge played freely with the Oxford forms. Christ Church has

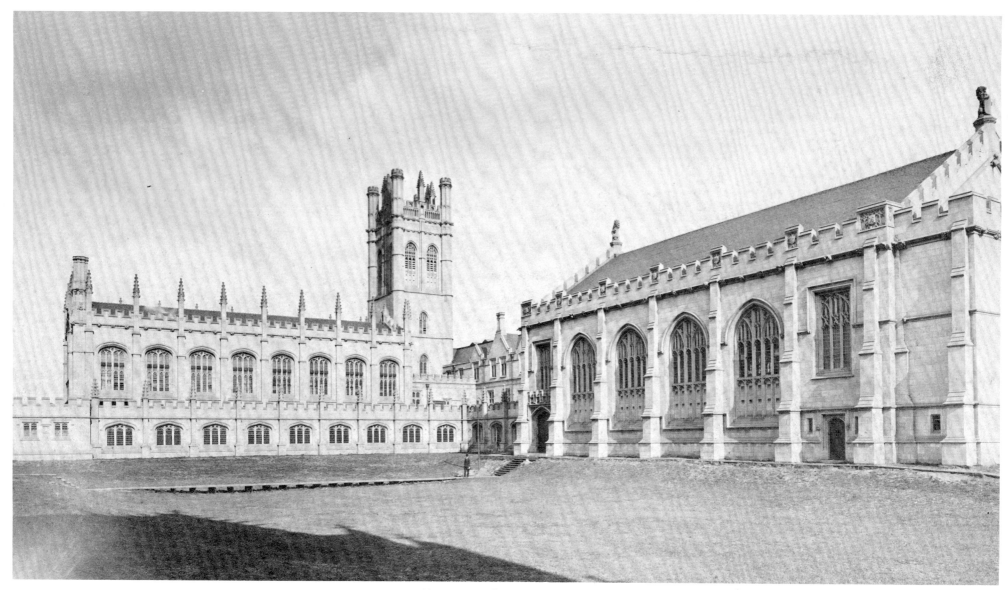

Tower Group from the south

ASSIMILATION OF GOTHIC FORMS, 1901–1916

Magdalen College Tower, Oxford

Reynolds Club and Mandel Hall from the east

a heavy squat tower. Mitchell Tower, derived from the tower of Magdalen College, rises majestically to signal the approach to the campus. In the Reynolds Club, as well, the adaptation is free; it is the use of the oriels and mullioned windows rather than their exact number, size, or placement that suggests St. John's. The chapel-like form of Mandel Hall[10] is adapted to the sloping auditorium floor by making the lower third of the great arched windows blind. [11]

Coolidge's handling of Gothic differs in many ways from that of Cobb. His roofs are lower and less sharply peaked. [12] There are no dormers and few gables. The windows are usually arched rather than square-headed, and divided by vertical mullions culminating in tracery at the top. The masses are much simpler. But he tips his architectural hat to Cobb in several courteous gestures. The lions atop the north and south gables of Mandel Hall respond to the griffins in the Hull group. The use of flat-topped turrets at the corners of Mitchell Tower instead of the peaked spires of Magdalen puts it at one with the tower of Ryerson Physical Laboratory. And Coolidge, too, like Cobb, emphasizes the ornamentation around entrances.

CHAPTER 10

CHARLES HITCHCOCK HALL

W hen Mrs. Charles Hitchcock proposed to give the University a men's
dormitory in memory of her husband,
Hutchinson encouraged Coolidge to submit
sketches, and the Committee on Buildings and
Grounds recommended that he be selected as architect for Hitchcock Hall. [1]

Mrs. Hitchcock had her own ideas, however, both
as to how the dormitory should be built and who
the architect should be. She was determined that
the dormitory should provide the comforts of a
home-like atmosphere for undergraduates and that
it include not only living units but a sitting room,
library, breakfast room, infirmary, and quarters for
the visiting preacher; [2] and she was equally determined that the architect be Dwight Heald Perkins. [3]

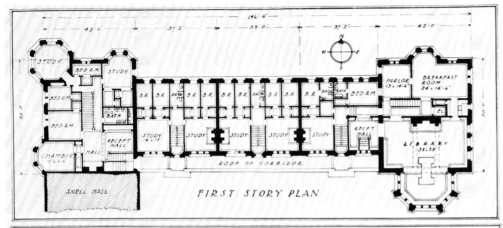

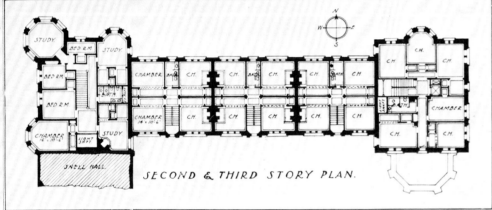

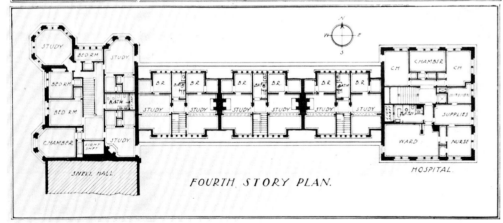

Hitchcock Hall floor plan, Dwight Heald Perkins, supplement to The Western Architect, *November 1903. Courtesy of The Art Institute of Chicago.*

On learning that Coolidge had been selected, she wrote Harper, "I am not content that the building should be put up as *my* expression of an adequate memorial for my husband, and as *my* ideal of what a boy's dormitory should be, when I have not been consulted at all."[4]

Harper was impressed with her ideas and with Perkins's preliminary plans, and in September 1900 Perkins too went abroad and visited Oxford in order to study its living arrangements.

In Hitchcock Hall, completed in 1902, Perkins availed himself, as Coolidge did, of certain elements of Oxford architecture which he then reworked to meet the demands of the building problem within a design that was essentially individual and highly original. But he was also aware, as was Coolidge, of the need for harmony between his building and the rest of the campus.[5]

He took from Oxford the concept of small living units, reached by separate entries, eliminating the long dark corridors used in the University's earlier barrack-like structures. Suites of two bedrooms and a study had fireplaces. There were five baths to a

Hitchcock Hall from the south

floor, as compared to one in the earlier men's dormitories. [6] Working around his basic floor plan, he incorporated various Gothic elements: carved stone ornamentation, deep-set arched windows, dormers, a cloister, bay windows, finial-tipped buttresses, and a tower. But they were all used in new ways. The stone ornamentation took the form of a crisp geometrical pattern on the string course. Where Gothic carving typically derived from plant forms was used, the plants were those of the midwestern prairie. The horizontal bands of windows were punctuated by the entry lights. Above their transoms, the windows were filled with geometrically leaded glass with small tinted inserts. The dormers ranged in long low strips. The cloister, too, was long and low. The five-sided library bay makes a summary statement of the way Perkins reused the Gothic elements and combined them with the new: the buttressed corners topped with finials carved in plant forms; the pointed arched apertures; the deep-set windows with their stained and leaded glass.

Mrs. Hitchcock recognized the originality of the building in a speech of gratitude at the housewarming she gave for the workmen and their families:

Hitchcock Hall library bay

Hitchcock Hall entrance with prairie vegetation ornament by Richard Bock

Hitchcock Hall cloister

Hitchcock Hall from the northwest

"To have an architect who gave me the fruits of study and travel in perfecting his thoughts of what a young men's dormitory should be, to have the assistance of a sculptor who designed from the woods and fields about us and made the English Gothic into an American Gothic . . . has been a joy to me."[7]

But there are signs that Perkins took pains to achieve consonance with the surrounding buildings, particularly on the street side. On Ellis Avenue the bay on Hitchcock Hall corresponds to one on Snell Hall. The tower balances Mitchell Tower a block away. The window bands from Snell Hall to Hitchcock Hall are continuous, similar in height and size. The basements are of equal height. The roof melts easily into the Snell Hall gable. Like the various buildings of Oxford, Hitchcock Hall and its neighbors are dissimilar but of a kind.

CHAPTER 11

QUESTIONING THE STYLE

Describing the amazing growth of the University for *Scribner's*, Professor Robert Herrick wrote, "The University has done more than grow; it has sprung into existence full-armed. And one benefit of this supernatural birth is that its external form has been planned with regard for the ensemble."[1]

As the University expanded beyond the quadrangles, however, the question arose as to whether or not it was time to abandon the commitment to the Gothic style and Bedford limestone. The problem was faced for both the School of Education and Bartlett Gymnasium.

The architect for the School of Education was James Gamble Rogers.[2] When the Chicago Institute merged with the University of Chicago in 1901,

Emmons Blaine Hall from Scammon Court, James Gamble Rogers, 1903

Emmons Blaine Hall from the Midway

the agreement stipulated that the University erect a building according to plans already prepared by Rogers for the Institute. [3] Harper intended to incorporate the Institute into a school of education on its own quadrangle that would include a graduate department of education, a college of education for undergraduates, elementary and secondary schools for teacher training, a laboratory school, the Chicago Manual Training School, and a secondary school. Rogers's plans, however, could not have accommodated so many diverse needs, and the cost would have been greater than anticipated.

The University worked with Rogers to reduce the price, requesting estimates on wooden joists and beams.[4] The cost of the building exteriors could not be reduced, however. A supply of bricks, already purchased for the Institute building, had been included in a $1,000,000 gift as part of the merger agreement. The matter was resolved when the Board of Trustees asked the Chicago Institute and John D. Rockefeller to appropriate an additional $50,000 so that the buildings could be made completely fireproof and constructed of stone instead of brick.[5] In spite of the additional appropriation, the University incurred a $23,000 loss on the project. When the University sold the bricks, it discovered they had been overvalued in the merger agreement.

The land for the education quadrangle was a square block on the Midway, two blocks east of the main campus, obtained, partly by purchase, partly by gift, from the widow of Jonathan Y. Scammon.[6] The first two buildings were Emmons Blaine Hall, which housed the elementary school and the teacher training facilities, and Belfield Hall, in which were placed the high school and the manual training school.

Emmons Blaine Hall (1903) was named for the late husband of Anita McCormick Blaine, founder of the Chicago Institute.[7] It was built as the southern component of a group that would eventually compose a quadrangle devoted to primary and secondary education, teacher training, and educational research. Although the Midway front was four stories high, the east and west wings were lower to allow the prevailing western breezes to enter the court. Most of the classrooms faced south, the windows grouped to avoid the appearance of a factory.[8] The first floor rooms opened onto a terrace where the children could plant gardens. Belfield Hall, forming the northern end of the quadrangle, consisted of two three-story, steeply gabled buildings joined by a long one-storied building housing the manual training shops.[9]

Even though the School of Education was two blocks from the main campus, the continuity of its architecture with the other University buildings gave it status and dignity. Using stone instead of brick meant a financial sacrifice for the University,[10] but the conformity of its buildings to the University's

Belfield Hall, James Gamble Rogers, 1904

interpretation of the Gothic style confirmed its place as an integral part of the academic complex.

The University's commitment to Gothic was tested once again when trustee Adolphus Clay Bartlett offered to give \$125,000 for a men's gymnasium as a memorial to his son. [11] The drawings prepared by Shepley, Rutan and Coolidge included two buildings, one for physical culture and one for athletics. The Bartlett gift was redesignated for the physical culture building only, but the lowest bid still exceeded Bartlett's donation. [12]

John D. Rockefeller, Jr., a trustee since 1898, protested to President Harper that "the exterior of the building is far more elaborate and hence more costly than is necessary or wise. . . . Possibly this is necessitated by the style of architecture; if so it seems to me that a simpler style would not only be less costly but greatly to be preferred." [13] And to Andrew MacLeish, vice-president of the Board, Rockefeller wondered, "Is it wise to use the cathedral architecture in a gymnasium?" [14] MacLeish concurred that it was desirable that "new buildings to be erected in the quadrangle north of 57th Street be simpler and less expensive than those on the main campus . . . [but] exception in this case ought to be made with the building that is to stand just across the street from the beautiful group which is to be constructed at the South-West corner of 57th Street and Lexington [University] Avenue." [15]

Construction of the gymnasium finally got underway when Bartlett increased his subscription to \$150,000; John D. Rockefeller, Sr., designated \$60,000 from his \$2,000,000 fund; [16] and John D. Rockefeller, Jr.'s, qualms were assuaged in an interview with President Harper and Martin Ryerson at Forest Hill, Cleveland. [17]

As completed in 1904, the gymnasium was massive and simple, declaring its function clearly. The battlemented towers, ornamented entrance, and embellished string course tied it closely to the Tower Group across the street, and Bartlett Gymnasium set a tone for the great medieval towers that would mark the entrance to Stagg Field some ten years later.

Bartlett Gymnasium, Shepley, Rutan and Coolidge, 1904

West stands of Stagg Field, ca. 1914

CHAPTER 12

THE PLAN REVISED AND REFINED

During 1901 and 1902, the plan for the use and disposition of buildings was altered in a number of ways.[1] Two factors which prompted these changes were the University's land acquisitions and a reevaluation of the original quadrangles.

In 1898, Rockefeller and Field jointly gave the University the two blocks immediately north of the quadrangles, and this tract was made into an athletic field. Rockefeller, using the University's business manager as his agent, subsequently acquired and presented to the University all of the property facing the north side of the Midway Plaisance from Cottage Grove to Dorchester Avenue, and all the property bordering the Midway's south side, a process completed by 1907.[2]

This expansion meant that certain functions envisioned for the original quadrangles could now be moved to other locations. The intention that the corner quadrangles be lined with dormitories was abandoned; the gymnasium was shifted to the athletic field and, with the exception of the student facilities housed in the Tower Group, the quadrangles were henceforth reserved for academic use.

Redesigning the central quadrangles was precipitated by the need to construct a main, or general, library that would satisfy the academic requirements of departments and also allow for future expansion. The planning for this building plunged the University into a lengthy debate that involved the entire academic community as well as the trustees. The issue was the relationship between the general library, yet to be built, and the departmental libraries scattered throughout the University. Although the need for a centralized library was fully recognized, faculty, particularly in the sciences, insisted on maintaining libraries within their departments.

A compromise plan adopted by the senate in April 1900, allowed departments with laboratories to re-tain their libraries but required the others to transfer their books to the general library.[3] An amendment to the report suggested moving the library from Cobb's site at 58th Street and Ellis Avenue to another location.[4] The logic of this must have been that it would serve no useful purpose to put the library adjacent to the science buildings at the north end of campus.

The Joint Commission on Library Building and Policy, composed of trustees and faculty, was authorized to consult an architect and solicit the advice of librarians and educators.[5] The Commission's plan, developed in cooperation with the University architect, Charles Coolidge, placed the library on the Midway Plaisance, and connected it with bridges to projected buildings for history, modern languages, classics, law, divinity, and philosophy.[6] Each of these buildings would have its own library, yet be so attached to the main library as to make access as easy as possible.

This planning venture had three important results. First, it inaugurated a systematic approach to meeting the University's space needs.[7] In the winter of 1903 President Harper, at the request of the trust-

Aerial view showing addition of Tower Group, Bartlett Gymnasium, School of Education, Law School, and Press and Power Buildings, 1907.

ees, appointed Ernest DeWitt Burton chairman of the Committee on Buildings and Grounds of the University Council. [8] Burton consulted with faculty about their departmental needs, [9] made a survey of eastern colleges and universities, [10] meticulously recording his findings in little notebooks, [11] and solicited student opinion on such matters as seating arrangements. [12] Although money for the buildings was a long time coming, methods of preparing for them were being developed.

A second outcome of the 1902 planning effort was the proposed concentration of all of the buildings for the humanities and social sciences in the southern sector of the quadrangles. The educational program was continuing to shape the arrangement of the physical facilities.

Ernest DeWitt Burton, Chairman of the Committee on Buildings and Grounds of the University Council, later President of the University, 1923–1925

Burton's notes on campus buildings, 1903

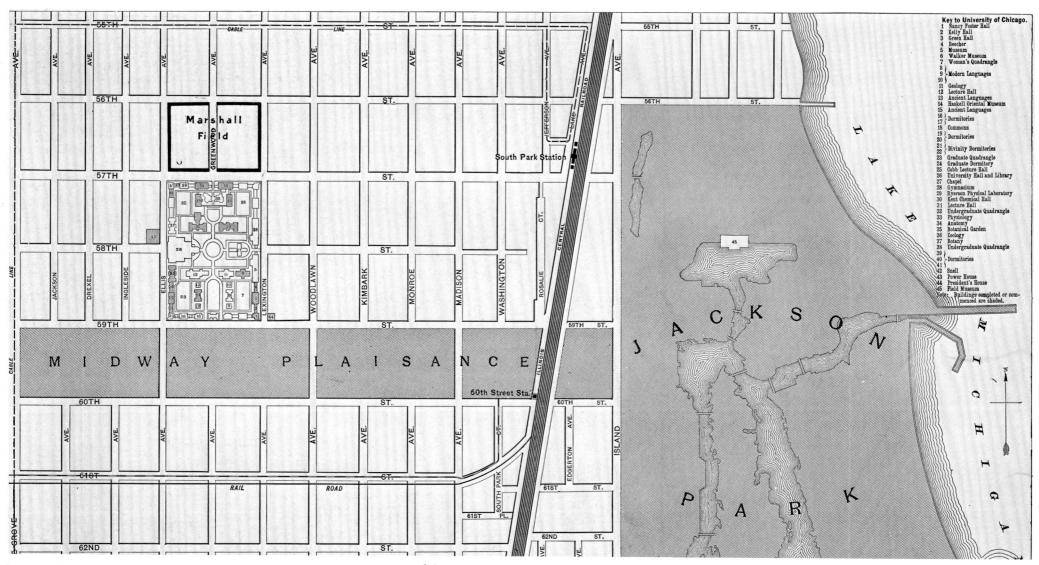

The key to University of Chicago map reads:

Key to University of Chicago.

1 Nancy Foster Hall
2 Kelly Hall
3 Green Hall
4 Beecher
5 Museum
6 Walker Museum
7 Woman's Quadrangle
8
9 Modern Languages
10
11 Geology
12 Lecture Hall
13 Ancient Languages
14 Haskell Oriental Museum
15 Ancient Languages
16
17 Dormitories
18 Commons
19 Dormitories
20
21 Divinity Dormitories
22
23 Graduate Quadrangle
24 Graduate Dormitory
25 Cobb Lecture Hall
26 University Hall and Library
27 Chapel
28 Gymnasium
29 Ryerson Physical Laboratory
30 Kent Chemical Hall
31 Lecture Hall
32 Undergraduate Quadrangle
33 Physiology
34 Anatomy
35 Botanical Garden
36 Zoology
37 Botany
38 Undergraduate Quadrangle
39
40 Dormitories
41
42 Snell
43 Power House
44 President's House
45 Field Museum
Note: Buildings completed or commenced are shaded.

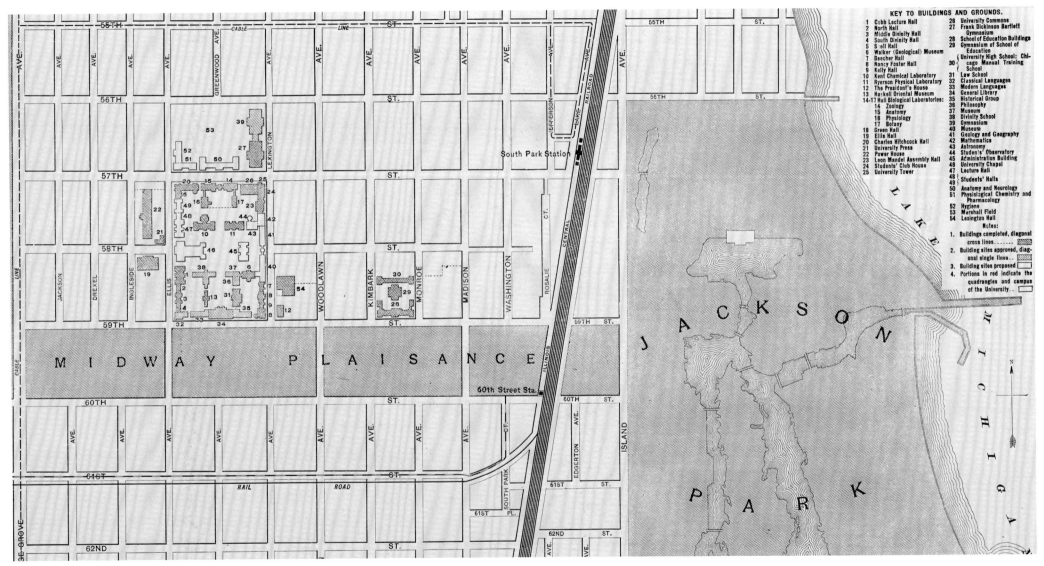

Map of the campus, University Register, *1902–3*

KEY TO BUILDINGS AND GROUNDS.

1 Cobb Lecture Hall
2 North Hall
3 Middle Divinity Hall
4 South Divinity Hall
5 Snell Hall
6 Walker (Geological) Museum
7 Beecher Hall
8 Nancy Foster Hall
9 Kelly Hall
10 Kent Chemical Laboratory
11 Ryerson Physical Laboratory
12 The President's House
13 Haskell Oriental Museum
14-17 Hull Biological Laboratories:
   14 Zoology
   15 Anatomy
   16 Physiology
   17 Botany
18 Green Hall
19 Ellis Hall
20 Charles Hitchcock Hall
21 University Press
22 Power House
23 Leon Mandel Assembly Hall
24 Students' Club House
25 University Tower

26 University Commons
27 Frank Dickinson Bartlett Gymnasium
28 School of Education Buildings
29 Gymnasium of School of Education
30 University High School: Chicago Manual Training School
31 Law School
32 Classical Languages
33 Modern Languages
34 General Library
35 Historical Group
36 Philosophy
37 Museum
38 Divinity School
39 Gymnasium
40 Museum
41 Geology and Geography
42 Mathematics
43 Astronomy
44 Students' Observatory
45 Administration Building
46 University Chapel
47 Lecture Hall
48 Students' Halls
49 Anatomy and Neurology
50 Physiological Chemistry and Pharmacology
51 Hygiene
52 Marshall Field
53 Lexington Hall
54

Notes:
1. Buildings completed, diagonal cross lines
2. Building sites approved, diagonal single lines
3. Building sites proposed
4. Portions in red indicate the quadrangles and campus of the University

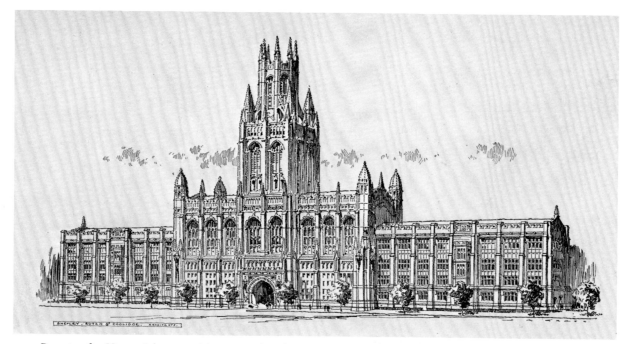

Drawing for Harper Library and history and modern languages buildings, Shepley, Rutan and Coolidge, 1906

A third and lasting effect was the orientation of the campus toward the Midway rather than inward upon itself. From this period forward the most important buildings would adorn the Midway front.

Only one building in the new plan was realized at the time, the Law School (1904). [13] With the death of President Harper in January 1906, the depression of 1907, and the fiscally conservative administration of Harper's successor, Harry Pratt Judson, building on the campus came to a halt. [14] The central building in the new plan, Harper Memorial Library, was not completed until 1912. Nevertheless, the plan held, and finally reached completion in 1929.

Harry Pratt Judson, President of the University, 1906–1922

Harper Memorial Library, Shepley, Rutan and Coolidge, 1912

CHAPTER 13

AN APPROPRIATE SYMBOLISM

Having adopted Gothic architecture and determined to stay with it, the University community gradually proceeded to translate the style's decorative forms into its own terms.

The Oxford buildings from which Charles Coolidge derived his inspiration were rich in sculptured ornament: canopied niches, shields, coats of arms, angels, heads of people, beasts, gargoyles, grotesques, and luxuriant plant forms. Christ Church, Magdalen College, and St. Johns all had string courses punctuated with small sculptured paterae, up high, and difficult to see, but creating an impression of lavish and imaginative embellishment. The fortress-like masses of Bartlett Gymnasium are enlivened with a variety of medieval beasts, monsters, and human heads. [1] The string courses of Hutchinson Commons, Mitchell Tower, and Mandel Hall carry similar carvings. They relate more closely to the beliefs and practices of the Middle Ages than to the University of Chicago.

There were, however, nascent signs that these motifs could be reworked to pertain to the buildings and their uses. Over the east door to Mandel Hall are two robed figures displaying a book, an apparent reference to the academic activities of the University. Scholars over the entrance to Mitchell Tower also hold books and scrolls. The Reynolds Club shield with its inscription "Sons of the Same Beloved Mother," is on its north wall. And over the door of the Law School appear kings and magistrates, guardians of order, and the scales of justice.

By the time Harper Memorial Library reached the design stage, faculty and trustees were taking an active part in the selection of symbolic ornament. Burton, after conferring with President Judson and members of the senate, presented for the approval of the Trustees' Committee on Buildings and Grounds a complex scheme involving the use of coats of arms and shields of European, American, and Asian universities and colleges, the marks of

Scholar over entrance to Mitchell Tower

Grotesque on cornice of Bartlett Gymnasium

Reynolds Club, Reynolds Club shield with motto,
"Sons of the Same Beloved Mother"

Figures with book, east entrance to Mandel Hall

Symbols of law over entrance to Law School

Harper Library reading room, west screen

Harper Library, west entrance

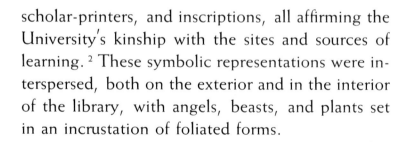

Classics Building, head of Cicero

Rosenwald Hall, geologists

scholar-printers, and inscriptions, all affirming the University's kinship with the sites and sources of learning. [2] These symbolic representations were interspersed, both on the exterior and in the interior of the library, with angels, beasts, and plants set in an incrustation of foliated forms.

Examples of the interplay between inscriptions, shields, and medieval motifs appear on the screens of the Great Reading Room. Under a frieze of grotesques, and set between niches with leafy can-

opies, the east screen carries the coats of arms of the universities of the Eastern Hemisphere: Oxford, Cambridge, Paris, Berlin, Petrograd, Bologna, Tokyo, and Calcutta. Above the screen is inscribed, "Whatsoever things were written aforetime were written for our learning." Its mate, the west screen, bears the coats of arms of universities of the Western Hemisphere: Harvard, Yale, Johns Hopkins, Columbia, Michigan, Wisconsin, California, and Chicago. Above is carved, "Read not to contradict nor to believe, but to weigh and con-

Rosenwald Hall, the geologists' motto, "Dig and Discover"

sider." The printers' marks carved on corbels underscore the University's identification with the transmission of knowledge. The double use of contemporary and medieval symbols is epitomized in the main entrance to Harper Library where an angel presides between the shields of the United States and the University.

With the Classics Building[3] (1915), Rosenwald Hall[4] (1915), and Ida Noyes Hall[5] (1916), a transition was made from medieval decorative themes to symbolic sculptures that expressed the activities within the buildings. At the central windows on the south elevation of Classics are the heads of Homer, Cicero, Socrates, and Plato. In the cornice are representations of Aesop's fables. Under the oriels, carvings depict the labors of Hercules. More of Aesop's fables appear at the north elevation, as well as a head of Seneca and a copy of an antique head in the Louvre. [6]

A committee composed of Thomas Chamberlin, Martin Ryerson, and Charles Hutchinson worked out the plan for Rosenwald Hall, built by Holabird and Roche to house the geology and geography departments. The shield above the main entrance

Ida Noyes Hall, knight in armor

Ida Noyes Hall, girl reading with a box of chocolates

is supported by students, one carrying a hammer, the other a surveying instrument. A frieze of roses alludes to the name of the donor. Relief portraits of Lyell and Dana flank the doorway. On the cornice are portrait heads of men eminent in the earth sciences, intermingled with crinoids, gastropods, coral, and sea urchins. Winged chimeras on the east tower in the forms of a buffalo, a bull, an elephant, and a lion represent America, Europe, Asia, and Africa. The octagonal tower, devoted to meteorology, has protruding figures representing the four winds and birds of the air. Near the tower entrance a panel bears a shield on which are carved a geologist's collecting bag and hammers, together with the legend, "Dig and Discover."[7]

The role of the women's building, Ida Noyes Hall, is conveyed through figures of young girls on the string course reading and playing, and, at the two corners, panels depicting the proverbial knights in shining armor. [8]

The University had created a Gothic symbolism of its own.

CHAPTER 14

THE UNION OF EXTERIOR AND INTERIOR

The second phase of the University's building program, starting with the Tower Group, marks the beginning of a studied effort to integrate the interior architectural elements, the decoration, and the furnishings with the buildings' exteriors.

The vaulted ceilings of the reading rooms of the Law School, Harper Library, and the Classics Building, the hammerbeams, paneling, and fireplaces of Hutchinson Commons, and the carved staircase and molded plaster ceilings of the Reynolds Club illustrate the architects' efforts to achieve a Gothic totality, inside and out. [1]

In interior decoration and furnishing, the University's Gothicism was fostered by the Arts and Crafts

Law School reading room

Harper Library reading room

Hutchinson Commons

movement then thriving in Chicago. English in origin and led by William Morris, a disciple of John Ruskin, the movement represented a rejection of industrialization and machine-made household objects and proposed a return to handcraftsmanship based on medieval designs and methods. Henry Hobson Richardson, Charles Coolidge's mentor, had been an early interpreter of the movement in America, and Coolidge himself had designed furniture in the Arts and Crafts manner. [2]

Like Richardson, Coolidge worked with an artist in developing the interior design, in this case Frederick Clay Bartlett, son of the donor of Bartlett Gymnasium. Bartlett was an accomplished muralist who had studied in Munich and Paris, and he brought the decorative arts into full play in both the gymnasium and the Tower Group. Describing his work he said, "The decoration of the new group of buildings has been dictated, to as great an extent as possible, by the architecture. The introduction of anything foreign in the way of color or design has been carefully avoided."[3]

Bartlett's mural for the gymnasium depicts an athletic tournament in the Middle Ages. His intent was to use both medieval subject matter and medieval method. In describing the mural he noted, "The crowd looking on at the games are in gorgeous holiday attire—brocades stiff with gold, cut velvets, and rich silks, with jewels of equal splendor. Many of the ornaments are raised in 'gesso' and gilded in antique gold leaf after the manner of the early English and Italian decorations."[4] The memorial window, on the great staircase, designed and executed by an associate of Louis Comfort Tiffany, Edward P. Sperry of New York, also depicts a medieval scene, Rowena crowning Ivanhoe. [5]

The chivalric life was readily translated into meaning for the present. As Frank Wakely Gunsaulus, local churchman and educator, said at the dedication, "The age is weary of vulgar and soul-destroying success. It longs for knightly devotion to what often seem lost causes in politics, society, church, and state."[6]

In the Tower Group, the walls and woodwork were carefully treated to suggest the mellowing of age, and the friezes in the library and billiard room were designed after studying old tapestries and fabrics. The small theater on the third floor of the Reynolds

Mural in Bartlett Gymnasium depicting a medieval tournament, Frederick Clay Bartlett, 1904

Stained glass window in Bartlett Gymnasium, Rowena crowning Ivanhoe, Edward C. Sperry, 1904

Reynolds Club theater curtain with medieval scene, Frederick Clay Bartlett, 1903

Hitchcock Hall library, molded ceiling by Richard Bock

Club had a painted curtain representing a fête day in medieval times. [7] The lighting fixtures, ordered from Tiffany, were designed to suggest the Gothic style. [8]

In the Hitchcock Hall library, completed in the same period as Bartlett Gymnasium and the Tower Group, the influence of the Arts and Crafts movement is also apparent, but the emphasis is not on medievalism itself but on its messages: references to natural objects, craftsmanship, simplicity, and a geometric rectilinear style. The frieze, a collaborative effort of sculptor Richard Bock and architect Dwight Perkins, combines vegetative forms with a flowing geometry. [9] Much of the furniture was designed by Gustav Stickley, a follower of Ruskin and Morris, who produced simple, sturdy, handcrafted oak chairs and tables as a revolt against ornate machine-carved Victorian furniture. The art glass lamps, leaded windows, and opaque drop-shaped lighting fixtures exemplify the application of handcraftsmanship to the decorative arts.

Charles Hutchinson, Martin Ryerson, and Mrs. Charles Hitchcock were in constant communication with the architects to make sure that every detail was perfect. The andirons for all of the fireplaces in the Tower Group, for instance, were designed by Shepley, Rutan and Coolidge at the request of Hutchinson and Ryerson, as were the mantel fixtures for the Commons. [10] Mrs. Hitchcock personally supervised the furnishing of Hitchcock Hall, enriching it with many of her own possessions, among them a portrait of William Morris purchased at his studio in Chelsea, and a portrait of Ruskin bought in Wales where he passed his last years. [11]

CHAPTER 15

THE SOCIAL VALUE OF TUDOR DOMESTICITY

In accepting Ida Noyes Hall from its donor, La Verne Noyes, President Judson said, "The beauty and comfort of this building I believe will enter permanently into the lives and characters of those who will here make their college home. It will enable them, I believe and trust, to have higher standards of life, which, wherever they may go and however simple the conditions of their lives, will give them ideals."[1]

Ida Noyes Hall, which provided for women the combined facilities that Bartlett Gymnasium, Hutchinson Commons, and the Reynolds Club offered men, was built after twenty-five years of compromises, failed plans, and dashed expectations. Efforts to share the men's quarters had been rebuffed early on. Responding in 1900 to a request for space

Ida Noyes Hall, Shepley, Rutan and Coolidge, 1916

for the Y.W.C.A. in the proposed men's club, President Harper regretted that it had been decided not to make arrangements for women there. "It is believed that, on the whole, better results will be gained by having a separate club house for women, which, perhaps, shall be connected with a gymnasium."[2] A temporary building for women, Lexington Hall, erected in 1903, was inadequate from the start. Completed plans for a women's quadrangle which would have contained dormitories, lecture rooms, a club house, gymnasium, and assembly hall were never executed.

When La Verne Noyes, a Chicago inventor and businessman, offered in 1913 to give the University a women's building in memory of his wife, Dean Marion Talbot and Gertrude Dudley, an assistant professor of physical culture, were already prepared with plans, which they presented to the Trustees' Committee on Buildings and Grounds.[3] Their goal, as Marion Talbot reported, was "to have every woman connected with the University share in the social life in such a way as to give expression to her individual qualities, to serve as hostess not only to other women but to men, and to give her training in forms of social expression which will make her

Drawing for Ida Noyes Hall cloister, Shepley, Rutan and Coolidge, 1914

academic training more effective as she mingles among people."[4]

Shepley, Rutan and Coolidge were engaged and the site selected. Although Talbot's choice had been the southwest corner of 58th Street and Woodlawn Avenue, due to its proximity to the lecture halls, libraries, and dormitories, the donor's preference for the 59th Street site was accepted. With the building of Harper Library, the University's Midway facade had become important, and a building as imposing as that being planned would be wasted tucked away in an inconspicuous location. [5]

A committee composed of representatives from the faculty, graduate and undergraduate women, and alumnae contributed to the plans. Several men were also consulted, including the president of the Reynolds Club and the president of the Dramatic Club. Together with a small committee of women faculty, Mrs. Judson and Mrs. Ryerson worked on the furnishings. [6]

While the exteriors of the first women's residences had been indistinguishable from the men's halls and classroom buildings, the new facility, built with the same Bedford limestone and red-tiled roof, was noticeably domestic. It resembled a Tudor manor house, even to the half-timbering and small gables at the rear. The windows were lacy and the ornament dainty. The great hall, with its broad iron staircase wrought in grapes and vines, its oak wainscoting and molded plaster ceiling, bespoke the hospitality Marion Talbot valued. The refectory, library, sun parlor, small meeting rooms, and theater were made to look like rooms in a luxurious home. It was the committee's idea to have the furnishings be a mingling of periods to simulate the accumulation of generations in an English country house. As Myra Reynolds remarked, "It was the theory that different periods could be used effectively together if the different pieces came from the same level of living and had a similar pedigree of culture and refinement."[7]

The dedication of Ida Noyes Hall was the climax of the Quarter-Centennial celebration. Again, a variety of women were involved, including an auxiliary committee with representatives of every class that had graduated since 1893 and two graduates of the Old University of Chicago. [8] The *Masque of Youth* was performed in the women's quadrangle

Ida Noyes Hall staircase

Rooms in Ida Noyes Hall, 1916

social rooms and theatre and gymnasium and swimming pool and dining rooms and all. At the reception, and the other university functions my college-honor of Aide made me still necessary to serve, so I felt very important and useful helping usher folks around.

They gave a Masque, called "The Gift" out on the campus, in honor of this famous new women's building. In it first an old man in gray robes appears: he is Gothic Architecture, and in a little speech he decides to settle here, and calls his spirits who are tall gray women with high Gothic headdresses and who dance stately "Gothic" dances. After that the people of the Masque parade in, led by a beautiful woman (an English professor) who is Alma Mater. She seats herself on a throne; and before her comes Youth, a curly-haired girl who dances a gay, mad dance,

and then goes and sits at Alma Mater's knee. Then before them come successively the dancers who impersonate the Lake, the Cloud and Rain, the Sun and the Moon. The Sun drives four figures ahead of him with golden reins, he and his "steeds" all in yellow; the moon is a woman in silver with a group of little children who gather moonbeams from her and dance and scatter them. The Cloud is a woman with billowy veils and the little rain-drops are children too. The Lake is a

Letter describing the Masque of Youth *performed at Quarter-Centennial Celebration, 1916*

Ida Noyes Hall mural, the Masque of Youth, *by Jessie Arms Botke; the* Spirit of Gothic Architecture
with page bearing University coat of arms followed by Alma Mater, 1918

before an audience of three thousand people. The *Masque,* which was led by the Spirit of Gothic Architecture, was later depicted in a mural in the third-floor theater, painted by Jessie Arms Botke. [9]

The splendor of Ida Noyes Hall disturbed President Judson. Its lavishness was justified, however, because it carried with it strong social, moral, and educational values. After the dedication, Professor Edith Foster Flint wrote him, "On the day of the Masque, last June, in speaking with me of Ida Noyes Hall, you said, 'Have we made it too beautiful?' And I remember that we agreed that its beauty ought to be educative in the best and most intimate sense of the word. . . . It is part of the work of English III to do some summarizing of various pieces of literature. . . . Among other bits I have assigned Ruskin's chapter on 'The Nature of Gothic'. . . . out of sixty-eight students in the past two years only one has elected it. But this year . . . eight chose that topic. And . . . in personal comment made it most emphatic that the campus buildings in general and Ida Noyes in particular had whetted their appetite for such knowledge and given them a new interest and pleasure. Now I am hoping to see aroused a like interest in interior decoration and comeliness of living and I believe it will come."[10]

PART III

GOTHIC'S FINAL EFFLORESCENCE
1926–1932

CHAPTER 16

BURTON'S DEVELOPMENT PROGRAM

E rnest DeWitt Burton became President of the University after Harry Pratt Judson resigned in February 1923. Although Burton had been anticipating retirement, he nevertheless threw himself into his new assignment with extraordinary energy and productivity, spearheading the University's largest building program to date. Between 1926 and 1932, twenty buildings were added to the campus, doubling the size of the physical plant. [1]

The University was entering a new period. The faculty had increased from 92 in 1893 to 603 in 1923, the student body from 510 to 12,745. [2] The work of the University was being hampered by a severe shortage of space and equipment. Plans for additional construction had been frustrated first by the onset of World War I and then by postwar inflation.

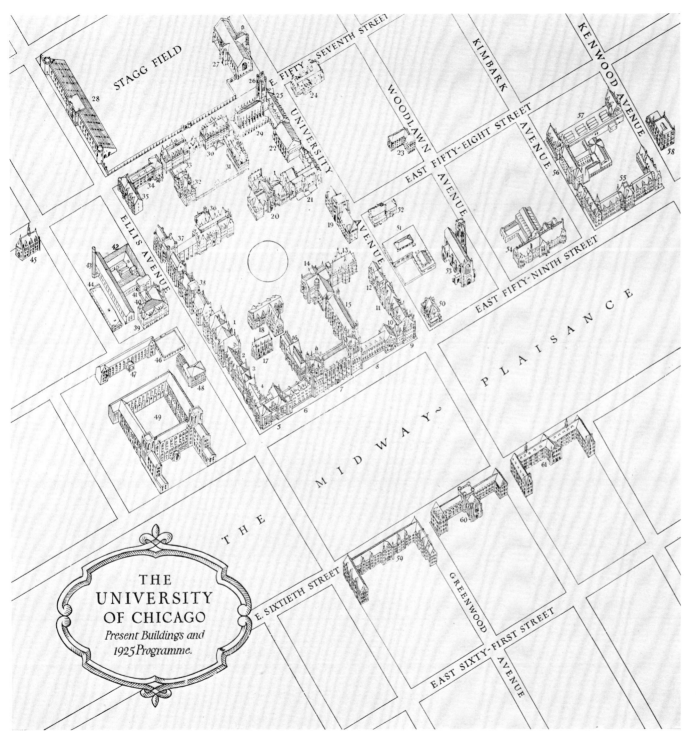

STAGG FIELD

E. FIFTY-SEVENTH STREET

KIMBARK AVENUE

KENWOOD AVENUE

WOODLAWN AVENUE

EAST FIFTY-EIGHT STREET

UNIVERSITY AVENUE

ELLIS AVENUE

EAST FIFTY-NINTH STREET

THE MIDWAY PLAISANCE

GREENWOOD AVENUE

E. SIXTIETH STREET

EAST SIXTY-FIRST STREET

THE
UNIVERSITY
OF CHICAGO
*Present Buildings and
1925 Programme.*

Isometric map showing plans for campus expansion, 1925

Great University Memorials,
designed to interest potential donors, 1925

The Sorbonne, University of Paris, derives its name from Robert de Sorbon, chaplain and confessor to Louis IX of France. He gave money in 1257 for the support of seven secular priests at the University and his name is often used for the whole university.

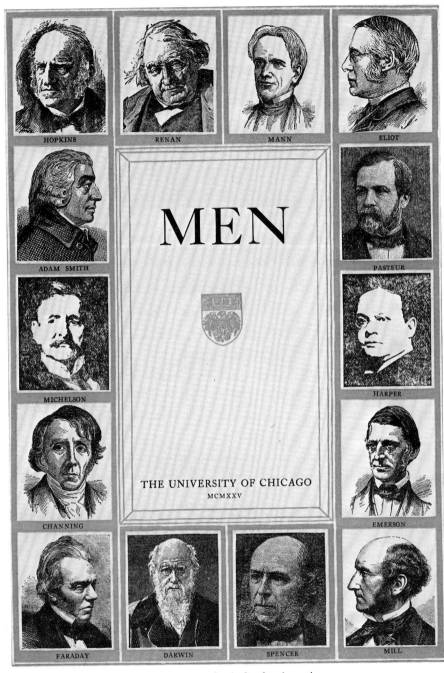

Men, *a brochure to raise funds for faculty salaries, 1925*

Burton seized the moment, and riding the wave of a new prosperity he started a campaign in 1925 to raise $11,000,000 for buildings and equipment and $6,500,000 for endowment. He estimated that by 1940 it would be necessary to have raised an additional $16,500,000 for buildings and $26,925,000 for endowment.[3] A Committee on Development was organized to work with staff, faculty, trustees, and alumni. Even before the campaign opened, pledges had been received for almost $5,000,000. Publicity took the form of a brochure, *The University of Chicago in 1940*, detailing goals, needs, and growth for the next fifteen years; another publication, *Great University Memorials*, inviting donors to perpetuate their names; a pamphlet entitled *Men* that solicited funds for faculty salaries; addresses; articles; and even printed souvenir pictures of existing buildings.

The building program that emerged from Burton's successful efforts was shaped by a number of factors. First, he started with a long-range plan. Second, his emphasis was on the importance of research. With such obvious exceptions as the chapels, power plant, and student facilities, each building's spaces were tailored to meet the research

Souvenir pictures of the University, 1923

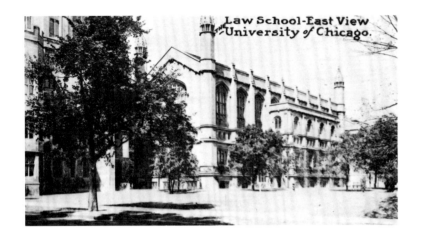

The Midway facade, The University of Chicago in 1940

needs of the faculty. Third, the University was now comfortable with its own image. It ranked in every field among the first four graduate schools in the United States.[4] Of the four Americans who had been awarded the Nobel Prize for science, three had done their major work at Chicago: A. A. Michelson, Alexis Carrel, and R. A. Millikan. The University was no longer looking to European models. As Julius Stieglitz, chairman of the Department of Chemistry, said, "Our universities are different from any type of university Europe has developed. . . . In my judgement there are inherent possibilities in the American university which could make it superior to any institution the older countries have developed."[5]

The University's fealty was now to its own past, its own campus, and its own continuity. Priority would be given to meeting the demands of the discipline to be housed. Buildings would harmonize with their predecessors but not allude specifically to Oxford or Cambridge.

The approach to building was systematized and refined to a stage well beyond the little notebooks Burton used to gather data for Harper Library. Ly-

man R. Flook, formerly superintendent of buildings and grounds, was made superintendent of construction, thus relieving the Trustees' Committee on Buildings and Grounds from the burden of innumerable details.[6] Emery Jackson, who had previously been with Shepley, Rutan and Coolidge and was largely responsible for Ida Noyes Hall, was retained first as a consultant and then as the University architect to prepare studies of the requirements for each building.[7] Many problems relating to the buildings and their equipment were now worked out among the University architect, the superintendent of construction, the business manager, and a faculty representative of the department concerned, and their solutions were then presented for approval to the trustees.

The Trustees' Committee on Buildings and Grounds continued to be the chief arbiter of the appearance of the buildings, deciding all questions of site, design, and choice of architect. The membership of this committee had remained remarkably stable. Although Charles Hutchinson, who had been one of its most influential members, died in 1924, Martin Ryerson continued to serve and to be consulted on all matters of significance. Thomas E. Donnelley, who replaced Hutchinson as chairman, had been a member since 1909, as had Harold F. McCormick. [8] Howard G. Grey had served since 1913. Robert L. Scott and Harold H. Swift were the most recent appointments, Swift in his capacity as chairman of the Board of Trustees. [9] He had, however, been a trustee since 1914 and was therefore thoroughly acquainted with the philosophy of the building program.

Even as the far-reaching plans for the future were being explained to the public, the University was constantly recalling its past. Goodspeed's biographies of benefactors appeared regularly in the *University Record* alongside departmental histories and biographies of noted faculty. The buildings that were erected reveal a desire to remain in consonance with the past while making those changes that would accommodate the present and welcome the future.

Although Burton died in 1925, before he could see his plans completed, the magnitude of his vision and the momentum of his campaign carried the building program forward and sustained it through the first years of the depression.

CHAPTER 17

THE PLAN BROUGHT TO COMPLETION

With the building of the Theology Group (1926), Wieboldt Hall of Modern Languages (1928), and the Social Science Research Building (1929), the south quadrangles were completed in accord with Charles Coolidge's plan made at the beginning of the century. Although there had been no new building on campus since the opening of Ida Noyes Hall in 1916, the University was secure in the knowledge that in time buildings would rise in their appointed places and be architecturally appropriate.

The Theology Group—Swift Hall and Bond Chapel—completed the enclosure of three quadrangles: Harper Court, the southwest quadrangle, and the great central quadrangle. The very placement of the Theology Group was symbolic. Burton

Model of the campus displayed at the Louisiana Purchase Exposition, St. Louis, 1904, showing the chapel and divinity school buildings on their present site

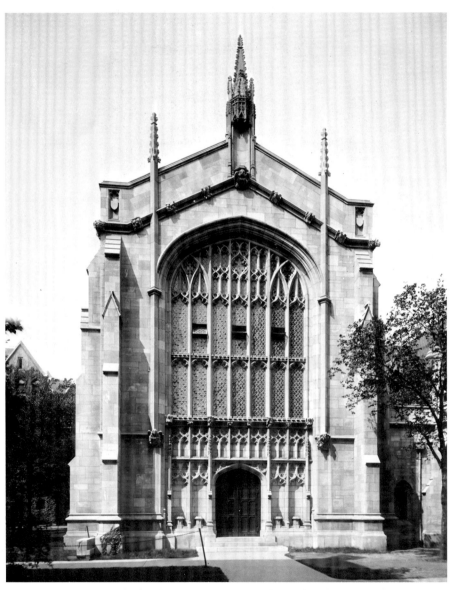

Joseph Bond Chapel, east entrance, Coolidge and Hodgdon, 1926

remarked that he was glad that "it stands near the center of the main quadrangle, because this suggests at least that the place of religion among the many interests of life is central."[1] By locating it adjacent to Haskell Oriental Museum and close to Classics and the projected social science building, the University was giving physical shape to Harper's conviction that the study of sacred scriptures was "associated with the study of the philology and literature of great nations of antiquity, as well as with psychology, and with the history and sociology of the past, in a sense perhaps in which no other subject has connection with these topics."[2]

Thomas E. Donnelley, Shailer Mathews, dean of the Divinity School, and Edgar Goodspeed, chairman of the Department of New Testament and Early Christian Literature, were appointed a special committee to confer with the architects on designs for both the theology building and Bond Chapel.[3] Goodspeed, as a young man, had visited the site of the new University with his father, studied with Harper at Yale, and joined the Divinity School faculty in 1898. Planning for the new buildings was both an expression of his love and loyalty for the institution with which he had spent his life and an

Cloister connecting Bond Chapel and Swift Hall, Coolidge and Hodgdon, 1926

Swift Hall, Coolidge and Hodgdon, 1926

opportunity for the exposition of the New Testament to which he had dedicated all his powers.

Joseph Bond Chapel is a small, beautifully proportioned building devoted solely to worship. A cloister connects it with the educational and research activities of Swift Hall, which houses the Divinity School. [4] In concept, size, and execution it is perfectly suited to its Gothic style. Its rich symbolism is expressed through exterior carvings, interior ornamentation, inscriptions, and stained glass windows.

On the west front are figures of Adam and Eve with snake and apple. Around the cornices are figures of evil: demons, griffins, and grotesques. On the east, inviting the worshiper into the Chapel, are musical angels and a medieval good shepherd. [5]

Within, the carving presents a wealth of Christian imagery. The narthex screen depicts birds among vines and grapes, a reference to the vine and branches of the Fourth Gospel. Polychrome hammerbeam angels, angels playing musical instruments, and cherubs ring the ceiling. The Matthean Beatitudes are carved into a frieze at the top of the

oak wainscoting. The eagle-borne lectern has both apocalyptic and evangelical connotations, and on the altar are carved the urn of memory and peacocks, symbols of hope for immortality.

The brilliant chancel window was designed by Charles J. Connick of Boston in cooperation with Goodspeed. [6] Although Connick professed to admire the work of John La Farge and the men who were in Tiffany's atelier, he deplored the opalescent pictorial window. He intended to make windows that were related to the architecture of the building and that were purveyors of light rather than solid walls of painted scenes. The subtlety and delicacy of the chancel window are in keeping with the intimate scale of the Chapel, enhancing rather than overwhelming it. [7]

As the Theology Group delineated the inner quadrangles, Wieboldt Hall and the Social Science Research Building filled in the Midway facade. It was more difficult, however, to relate the latter two buildings to neighboring structures. Unlike the free-standing Theology Group, each linked two other buildings: Wieboldt Hall joined the Classics Building with Harper Library; the Social Science Research Building occupied the space between Harper Library and Foster Hall. Both the modern languages and social sciences departments wanted buildings that would function as laboratories, reflecting the strong research orientation of the University.[8] They needed office space, storage areas for data and equipment, seminar and reading rooms, cubicles for graduate students, and, most of all, bookstack space for Harper Library's overflowing shelves. The problem was to avoid a factory-like appearance and maintain continuity with the elaborate and imposing structure of Harper Library.

Architectural plans for both Wieboldt Hall and the Social Science Building were redrawn. The first version of Wieboldt Hall was revised with more and larger windows, six small dormers instead of three large ones, provisions for fireplaces, and a reorganized and more tightly composed entrance. The drawing for the Social Science Building was modified according to Martin Ryerson's suggestions. The architects were requested to "redesign the upper facade, substituting a battlement treatment with retention of the dormer windows, and lowering the arc of the arch of the top tier of windows, simplifying or possibly removing entirely the

Angels at entrance to Bond Chapel

Cherubim
Love

Seraphim
Wisdom

Joseph
Sq,Lilies
rod

Powers   Virtues   Thrones   Dominions Principalities

Sword   Keys   Shell

Mary   Lazarus   Martha
Oint.   Phoenix   Fruit

Thomas Philip   John Bap   Simon   Mathias
Sq,arrows,Loaves   Lamb,Bk   Fish   hatchets.

Eliz, Gates   Zech. censer

*Chancel window symbolism indicated
by the designer, Charles J. Connick,
1928*

Wieboldt Hall, Coolidge and Hodgdon, 1928

Social Science Research Building, Coolidge and Hodgdon, 1929

tracery in them. This was for the purpose primarily of lowering the apparent height of the building to correspond more closely with the height of Wieboldt and Classics. . . . [This] will undoubtedly result in improved building design."[9]

The Gothicism which served Bond Chapel so naturally was less easily expressed in these linking buildings. Ryerson's long experience with the building program as well as his aesthetic acumen assured the consonance of these buildings.

CHAPTER 18

GOTHIC AND THE DEMANDS OF SCIENCE

A medical school and hospital were high on Burton's list of priorities. When it appeared that these facilities would actually be built, the appropriateness and economic feasibility of the Gothic style were seriously questioned.

Planning for a medical school that would train physicians and serve as a major research center started with the affiliation President Harper established with Rush Medical College in 1898 and the transfer of the first two years of instruction in medicine to the University campus. It was not until 1916, however, that plans for a development campaign for medicine were set forth. With the encouragement of the Rockefeller Foundation, the University sought to raise funds for an undergraduate medical school on the Midway, a teaching hospital with laboratories

Model for Billings Hospital, Coolidge and Hodgdon, 1919

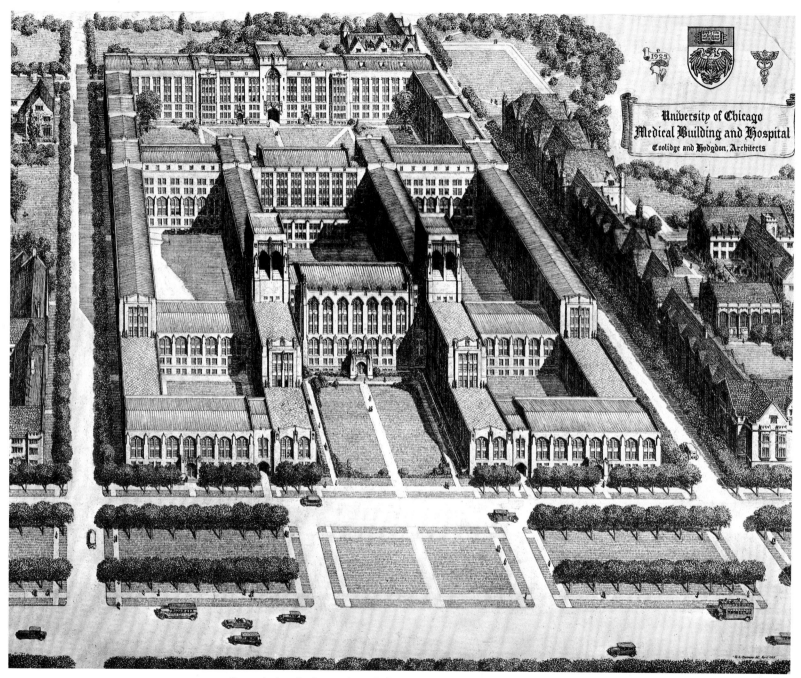

Revised plan for hospitals and clinics, Coolidge and Hodgdon, 1925

and lecture rooms, and a graduate school on Chicago's west side in affiliation with Rush Medical College and Presbyterian Hospital. Both medical school and hospital were to be run by a full-time salaried staff, an innovative approach that would establish in the Middle West a medical center comparable to that of Johns Hopkins in the East. The estimated cost for buildings and endowment was $5,000,000. Dr. Frank Billings, who had been dean of Rush and professor of medicine at the University, persuaded his family to contribute $1,000,000. The General Education Board and Rockefeller Foundation each offered $1,000,000 provided the balance could be raised. [1]

Charles Coolidge was the obvious choice to design the hospital and medical school. His firm had extensive experience designing hospitals, laboratories, and medical schools, including those for the Rockefeller Institute in New York, Princeton, and Peking, for Harvard and Western Reserve, and a number of Boston hospitals. Coolidge was appointed architect for Billings Hospital in January 1918. [2] Characteristic of the University's relationship with Coolidge, the agreement was oral, with Hutchinson and Ryerson taking full personal responsibility for the University's interests. [3]

Dr. Ralph Seem, who had been acting superintendent of Johns Hopkins Hospital, was appointed director of Billings Hospital in 1919. Dr. Winford Smith, superintendent of Johns Hopkins, was retained as an adviser. [4] The first sketches, in 1919, by both Coolidge and Smith, were for a medical center south of the Midway, but questions of style and materials were held in abeyance. President Judson, reporting to Ryerson on a conference with Billings, Smith, Seem, Coolidge, and Coolidge's Chicago partner, Charles Hodgdon, wrote, "It is questionable whether a hospital can advantageously involve the Gothic forms. It would seem to me desirable, however, to retain on the South Side of the Midway the grey stone and red tile roofs, otherwise buildings there would seem to belong to different institutions." [5]

Smith also objected to Gothic, stressing to Hodgdon, "I did not favor Gothic architecture for the hospital buildings, and I wish now to go on record to that effect. . . . I think it is more extravagant in the cost of construction and more difficult to obtain desirable fenestration." [6]

Despite these objections, the model approved by the trustees was decidedly Gothic. [7] Once estimates were prepared, however, the report was tabled.[8] Business manager Wallace Heckman observed that "a resurvey of important assumptions may be necessary. Is it certain that the present monumental Gothic stone type of structure, at a cost with equipment of between $5,000,000 and $6,000,000 is the essential first step? Dr. Jordan and other research men state that for their work Ricketts Laboratory South [a one-story brick building] is more available than the same space in the more substantial buildings."[9]

The urgency of the new building program made a final decision imperative. Heckman was unswerving, relating the views of a distinguished English physiologist on the University's Department of Physiology, "Isn't it too bad that they are housed in such a building as this [Culver]? They should be in a factory type building where they can have all the light they need."[10]

The chairman of the Board of Trustees, Harold Swift, appealed to Ryerson and Hutchinson, still the authorities in matters of taste, to reconsider the medical project. Many science faculty opposed locating the complex south of the Midway and argued in favor of maintaining contiguity of departments. And perhaps, too, the buildings should be redesigned in a Classic style for the sake of economy.[11] Ryerson replied firmly, "The proposal to change our style of architecture does not strike me favorably at first glance."[12]

In January 1925, Coolidge presented revised plans for a medical complex on the north side of the Midway which maintained a Gothic exterior without compromising the needs of a medical facility, explaining that the designs were "notably Gothic . . . but . . . the modern interpretation of the school, more modern than that of Harper Library."[13]

The five buildings to be erected were planned to function as independent but closely connected units. The first courtyard contained an administrative building, set back from the Midway, that joined the surgical and medical buildings. At the north end these were connected by the pathology building. North of that a free-standing structure housing physiology, pharmacology, and surgical chemistry formed the first unit of what would become the medical students' court. This area was accessible to

Billings Hospital, Coolidge and Hodgdon, 1927

Hospitals and clinics with adjoining units, 1931

campus science buildings, while public entrances to the hospital and clinics were on the Midway side. The two large square towers on Billings Hospital, echoing those of Harper Library, housed elevator machinery and water tanks. [14]

The Gothic feeling was derived from an architectural calligraphy in which various Gothic devices were recombined and patterned upon the facade: narrow niches, niches set into shallow buttresses, stylized tracery etched on the towers and parapet. As other hospital units were added, they conformed to the general architectural style of Billings and to the courtyard plan, perpetuating the unity of effect so valued by the Trustees' Committee on Buildings and Grounds.

CHAPTER 19

MODERN GOTHIC AND THE CHAPEL BLOCK

When it was dedicated on October 28, 1928, the long-awaited chapel was the University's largest and most elaborate building. In it can be seen a reinterpretation of Gothic that makes it very much a structure of its own time. Designed by Bertram Grosvenor Goodhue and erected after his death by his associates Mayers, Murray and Phillip, it is as different from Coolidge's buildings as Coolidge's were from Cobb's. The Oriental Institute (1931), also the work of the Goodhue Associates, forms a portion of what was originally conceived as a chapel block of complementary buildings connected by cloisters.

When John D. Rockefeller made his final gift of $10,000,000 to the University in 1910 he stipulated that at least $1,500,000 be used to erect and furnish a University chapel. [1] In 1918, on the recommendation of President Judson, Ryerson, and Hutchinson, Goodhue, a leading American designer of ecclesiastic Gothic, was selected as architect. [2] For Goodhue, profoundly influenced by Sir Giles Gilbert Scott, designer of Liverpool Cathedral, the chapel commission presented an opportunity to work toward what he referred to as "Modern Gothic."[3]

Goodhue prepared preliminary sketches for a chapel block just west of Ida Noyes Hall which included a general block plan, a perspective of the chapel from the west, and a sketch of the interior showing the tower over the crossing. The chapel faced south, further to enhance the view from the Midway. When the estimates came in, however, they were so far in excess of the allotted sum that Goodhue was requested to incur no further expense until he heard from the Committee on Buildings and Grounds. [4]

Goodhue reopened the matter in 1923 with three revised drawings, [5] including one showing the tower over the west transept. Goodhue felt that this was both more economical and a distinct improvement

Drawing for a University chapel interior, Bertram Grosvenor Goodhue, 1920

MODERN GOTHIC AND THE CHAPEL BLOCK 153

Drawing for a University chapel from west, Bertram Grosvenor Goodhue, 1920

Revised drawing for a University chapel with transeptal tower, Bertram Grosvenor Goodhue, 1923

Max Mason, President of the University, 1925–1928

artistically.[6] Early in 1924, President Burton called on Goodhue in New York, hoping that a plan could be made for a chapel alone that would come within the available sum. He had doubts about the design. "We do not want a building like St. Vincent's on Lexington Avenue. It is too cold and hard and without charm. We shall have to be on our guard lest Goodhue give us too plain and massive a building. . . . Will sculptured figures give as much charm as conventional carving?" he wrote Donnelley.[7] Burton, accustomed to Coolidge's foliated carving, crenellations, and embellishments, was uneasy with Goodhue's interpretation of the Gothic which emphasized "finely proportioned solids and surfaces devoid of all detail except that of noble sculpture."[8]

After Goodhue's death in 1924, the question arose as to whether the University should continue with his associates or find a new architect. Burton consulted Coolidge, who assured him that in the "Goodhue Chapel we have the work of a great architect, the greatest master of Gothic in America or England in this generation."[9]

Burton remained uncertain, however, and in August

University Chapel from the south, Goodhue Associates, 1928

he made a tour of England reminiscent of Hutchinson's earlier trip to Oxford, seeking precedents for the tower at the end of the transept, the high clerestory windows and low side aisles, and the immense forty-foot bays that were features of Goodhue's design. He found none for the first, few for the second, and only one example for the third: Liverpool Cathedral, itself a "modern" Gothic building, the work of a "daring modern architect," Sir Giles Gilbert Scott. [10] Bolstered by an interview with Scott, Burton concluded in his report on the trip that the "Goodhue plan was practicable and good in all its essential features and dimensions." [11]

Burton died in 1925, and Max Mason became President of the University. In that capacity Mason served on the chapel committee on symbolism. [12] The committee tried to select figures that would show how all human experiences merge in a universal religion. [13] The sculptured figures by Lee Lawrie, Edward Ardolino, and Ulrich Ellerhusen include the great leaders that form the march of religion in the south frieze; disciples, apostles, and saints flanking the Te Deum window; and figures to represent philosophy, science, literature, music, statesmanship, and architecture, as well as such

University Chapel, interior,
Goodhue Associates, 1928

Oriental Institute, Mayers, Murray and Phillip (formerly Goodhue Associates), 1931

Oriental Institute interior

abstract concepts as truth, strength, mercy, righteousness, peace, and beauty. [14]

The tiled vaulted ceiling is richly ornamented with color. Goodhue wanted the windows to be of cathedral glass in amber and purple shades so that the color effects could come from the ceiling. [15] The starkness of the great pale windows and masonry walls is relieved by ornate woodcarving on the reredos, organ screens, choir stalls, and canopies.

The University chapel resembles a medieval cathedral, as Goodhue said, in that "its buttresses 'butt' "; [16] the only structural steel is in the balconies, tower, and roof. In other ways, however, it is of its own period: the clean simple lines of the massed masonry, the strong piers, the geometric precision of the stepped gablets on the buttresses, the sculptured figures that seem to grow out of the stone, and the contemporary symbolism mark it as a twentieth-century building. Its name was changed to Rockefeller Chapel after the death of its donor in 1937.

As the chapel neared completion the Rockefeller Foundation responded to James H. Breasted's appeal for a new and enlarged Oriental Institute, the collections having long since outgrown Haskell Oriental Museum. [17] Plans were prepared by Mayers, Murray and Phillip.

The plans were "studiously simple," and intended to set off the chapel without competing with it. [18] The Gothic elements—gables, dormers, buttresses, bays, and beams—mingle with the decorative features of "Art Moderne," now sometimes called Art Deco. It was a natural amalgamation, for Egyptian art had an important influence on Art Moderne, especially since the opening of Tutankhamen's tomb in 1922. Stylized Egyptian motifs grace the bronze gates and painted ceilings, giving the interiors a chic opulence unexpectedly made possible by the fact that the depression had placed the University in a "buyer's market in the building industry." [19]

Both the chapel and the Oriental Institute illustrate the ways in which the basic Gothic format was reinterpreted to accommodate itself to changes in aesthetic sensibility. The adaptability that had characterized Gothic in earlier centuries continued to serve it in these later years.

CHAPTER 20

PROBLEMS OF SIZE AND SCALE

Harper's vision of collegial housing remained unrealized for four decades. By 1924 only 640 undergraduates of 13,734 lived in dormitories, the others residing in fraternity houses, at home, or in boarding houses.[1] Concerned about the situation, President Burton declared, "We must provide residence halls for these students . . . and . . . so construct and conduct them that they shall be far more than dormitories. . . . They should be in effect colleges, fraternities in which there is a constant and healthful interchange of thought and development of friendships."[2] Vice-President Frederick Woodward added, "Too many of our students, when they leave the classroom, the library, or the laboratory, leave the real atmosphere of the University. Too many of them escape almost entirely the stimulating associations and wholesome

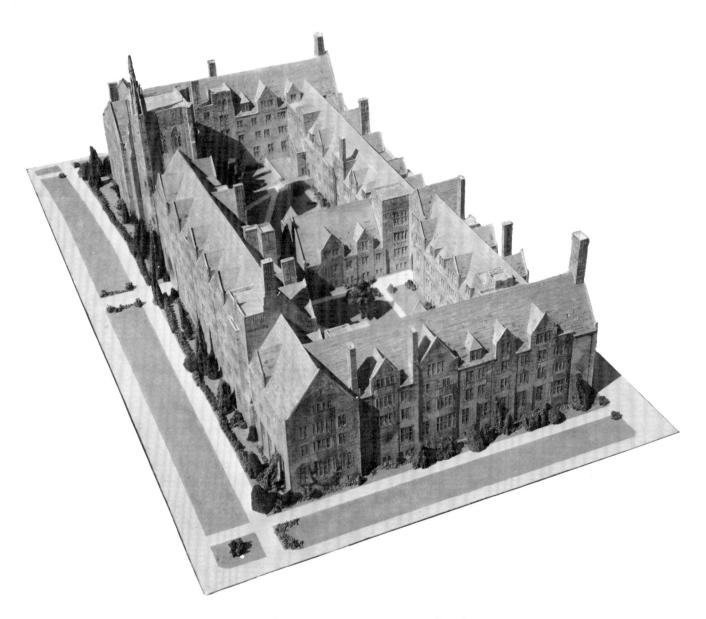

Model for men's residences Zantzinger, Borie and Medary, 1929

Burton-Judson Courts from the south, Zantzinger, Borie and Medary, 1929

influences which should play an important part in their education."[3]

In the late twenties Julius Rosenwald contributed money toward a men's residence, and John D. Rockefeller, Jr., offered to build and equip an International House. The number of people to be served by these two facilities was so great, however, that problems of size and scale had to be resolved if the buildings were to provide a congenial setting.

The men's residence, later named Burton-Judson Courts, was the first building erected south of the Midway. University planners recognized that the distance from the main campus would be a problem and proposed to solve it in two ways: by making the residence especially appealing and attractive, and by providing a connecting tunnel under the Midway.[4]

By the late twenties the term "Collegiate Gothic" referred, not as it had in the early part of the century to Oxford and Cambridge,[5] but to what had become an American architectural genre of its own. The English tradition had been subjected to an American interpretation, resulting in more regular-ity, more organization, and certainly more bathrooms. Lyman Flook and Frederick Woodward toured eastern colleges prior to planning for the new residence. The architects selected, Zantzinger, Borie and Medary, were known for their "medieval" work at Princeton, Yale, the University of Pennsylvania, and other institutions.[6]

Studies of housing requirements and possible financing led to the decision to build a dormitory that would house 400 men. A faculty committee surveyed other institutions and polled campus opinion. Its recommendations included two contiguous quadrangles, each housing approximately 200 men, buildings of the "entry" rather than "corridor" type, a preponderance of single rooms and some variety in size and rents, four dining rooms, common rooms, facilities for recreation, and suites for resident heads.[7]

The original model was carefully examined by the Trustees' Committee, resulting in a number of modifications: the tower, shorn of its pinnacle, was shifted from the east to the west end of the north face, presumably to correspond to Wieboldt Hall's tower across the Midway; the south wings, which were lowered to one story, were altered to include two dining rooms instead of four; and the club house, instead of being in the center was divided into two parts, each serving one quadrangle. The second stories of the club house wings were to contain libraries and conference rooms. [8]

The structure successfully met the goals of the building program within the Collegiate Gothic style. It provided intimacy and a meaningful communal life for a large group of men, and it was visually pleasing. [9]

For International House, the problems of size and scale were less easily solved. Unlike the Burton-Judson site, which is a full city block square, the area for International House, while a block long, was only a fourth of a block deep. The building, intended to house 525 American and foreign men and women, would have to be tall and narrow. In response to an inquiry about a possible design for International House, Harry Edmonds, director of the New York House, wrote, "it shouldn't be a skyscraper, for I do not think a tall building would harmonize with the prevailing architecture of the university community." [10]

The architects were Holabird and Root, successors of Holabird and Roche who had built Rosenwald Hall. [11] They were experienced in the design of hotels and commercial skyscrapers. They submitted sketches for the approval of John D. Rockefeller, Jr., and the Trustees' Committee. Rockefeller's reaction was general approval, although he felt that "perhaps a greater degree of harmonization between the Gothic aspects and the modern aspects might be an improvement." [12] The architects responded with sketches suggesting possible revisions, noting "there is very little precedent for a high building of this character." [13] The building was redrawn again in an effort to diminish the relative height of the north portion, and a solution was found much like that utilized in the medical center. Setbacks of varying heights provided an interesting composition and lessened the feeling of massiveness. A sense of intimacy was achieved with the treatment of the Midway facade, which minimized the necessary height, making it apparent only when viewed from the north.

Spaces for mingling in both small and large groups were provided: a large main lounge, an auditorium, small social rooms for men and women, meeting

Burton-Judson Courts from the Midway

Drawing for International House, Holabird and Root, 1930

The University of Chicago Builds a Student Home for Men, *1931*

Revised drawing for International House, Holabird and Root, 1932

International House from the north, Holabird and Root, 1932

International House Bulletin of Information, *1932*

rooms, kitchenettes where different nationalities could prepare their own dishes, a library, dining room, and a "modernistic" cafe which opened onto a landscaped courtyard. [14]

Furnishing new buildings had been, up to this time, handled by trustees, donors, or faculty committees in cooperation with the business office. But the immensity of the task of furnishing both the men's residence and International House led to both buildings being turned over to professional interior decorators. And, like the Oriental Institute, both benefited from the depression, which drove down prices and increased competition for work and commissions in what were at that time the largest private construction projects in Chicago. [15]

THE PERSISTENCE OF SYMBOLISM

During the earlier stages of the University's building program, sculptured ornament took traditional Gothic forms: shields, gargoyles, and grotesques; animals, fruits, and vines; kings, queens, and magistrates. These were in time augmented by carvings that were related to the function of the building, as on Harper Library, Rosenwald Hall, the Classics Building, and Ida Noyes Hall.

Later, the religious symbolism of Gothic architecture was readily adapted to the purposes of both Bond Chapel and Rockefeller Chapel. The architectural protocol for the other buildings erected in the twenties also included symbolic ornament; for each building the President of the University appointed a faculty committee on symbolism. [1] The committee's rationale was intellectual rather than religious or aesthetic, and the images ranged from depictions of academic disciplines to allegories.

On Wieboldt Hall, which houses the modern language departments, the traditional foliate carving is combined with lettering and three-dimensional heads. The south entrance is flanked by busts of two students in academic dress. In the spandrels above are two books bearing inscriptions, one from the first German Bible translated from the Greek, the other from the Strasbourg oath. Heads of writers decorate the cornice: Lessing, Goethe, Schiller, Ibsen; Dante, Molière, Hugo, Cervantes; Chaucer, Shakespeare, Milton, and Emerson. Between the heads are scenes from some of their writings. The ends of the window arches below are decorated with small figures from choir stalls in English cathedrals. [2]

Both the Social Science Research Building and Eckhart Hall display a combination of images and symbols illustrating aspects of their respective disciplines. In the spandrels of the arches of the north portico of the Social Science Building are bas-relief medallions of the heads of Smith, Gal-

Wieboldt Hall entrance

Wieboldt Hall cornice

ton, Gibbon, Bentham, Boas, and Comte. On the molding below the parapet are bosses on which are depicted labor, commerce, government, family, agriculture, history, the ballot, a calculating machine, and a slide rule and calipers. These bosses are repeated on the south side where, under the oriel, appears a paraphrase from Lord Kelvin's writings, "When you cannot measure . . . your knowledge is . . . meager . . . and . . . unsatisfactory."[3]

Eckhart has the same combination of Tudor Gothic vegetative ornament and sculptured medallions on either side of the entrance, in this case Newton and Gauss. Flat incised symbols on shields include the twelve signs of the zodiac and the proof for the Pythagorean theorem. In the arches over the entrances are carved arrangements of the names of men who made important contributions to mathematics, physics, and astronomy. At the west end of the north wing passageway are the shields of three European universities that influenced the development of mathematics in America: Göttingen, Paris, and Cambridge. [4]

Jones Chemical Laboratory, too, has its combination of portrait heads and flat symbols. [5] Willard Gibbs and August Kékulé, founders of modern physical and organic chemistry, are on either side of the east entrance; John Dalton is over the west

Social Science Building bosses depicting measuring and calculating devices

Social Science Building north portico with portrait reliefs of Smith and Galton

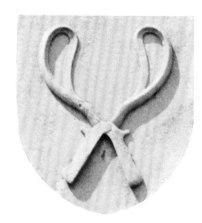

Chicago Lying-in Hospital, obstetrical instrument

Eckhart Hall south entrance with portrait reliefs of Newton and Gauss

International House entrance with relief depicting the gathering of peoples

door. Between the upper two tiers of windows are squares set in octagons on which are carved a Bessemer converter, symbolizing the fundamental connection between chemistry and industry, and such tools of the discipline as a balance, retort, and spectroscope. [6]

Hicks-McElwee Orthopedic Hospital is decorated with bas-relief rectangles containing names of prominent contributors to the field of orthopedics and shields of barbers' guilds. The cloister of Chicago Lying-in Hospital, designed by Schmidt, Garden and Erikson, has shields with the names of women's physicians, the center one being left blank for the discoverer of the cause of eclampsia. Low reliefs of child-birth instruments indicate the hospital's purpose. [7]

At another level of meaning are carvings with emblematic or allegorical significance. The central panel over the main entrance to International House symbolizes the gathering of peoples from the four quarters of the globe: North America, Europe, South America, and Asia. The bosses in the arch below are flowers of Russia, France, England, Canada, India, Japan, Egypt, and China. Over the

Oriental Institute tympanum

Dorchester Avenue entrance, the carving in the tympanum is a globe and steamship representing the passage of peoples from one part of the earth to another. The figures in the frieze below represent the different populations of the world. The corbels at the termination of the window moldings depict primitive man on one side and modern man on the other, and the bosses in the arch are a study of man's progress. Other carvings on International House pursue these same themes. [8]

The tympanum over the north entrance to the Oriental Institute, conceived by James Breasted and designed by Ulric Ellerhusen, suggests the interrelationships between East and West. The central figure on the left, or East, is an Egyptian scribe with a palette and writing kit over his shoulder. He stands among the ruins of a temple, having just given the figure from the West a wall fragment with the hieroglyphic inscription, "I have beheld thy beauty." This gift is meant to represent the Eastern origin of the Western writing system. Behind the central figures are symbols of Eastern and Western civilization. On the Eastern side are the Egyptian lion, the pyramids, the Sphinx of Kahfre, and the ruins of Persepolis. The great men of Eastern history are pictured from the top down in chronological order: Djoser, Hammurabi, Tuthmosis, Ashurbanipal, and Chosroes. On the western side are a bison, the Parthenon, a European cathedral, and the Nebraska state capitol designed by Bertram Goodhue. The six men representing the West are Herodotus, Alexander the Great, Julius Caesar, a crusader, a "modern excavator," and a "modern geologist." At the top of the tympanum and uniting the two spheres is a sun disk with the symbol of life and diverging rays terminating in human hands. [9]

The apparent incongruity of the symbolism on some of the buildings reflects the growing tension between the medieval idiom and the intellectual and artistic demands of a machine age. The traditional Gothic embellishment is supplemented with modernistic symbols of scientific advancement and social realist representations of the University's humanistic concerns. The result is a decoration that frequently seems contrived, striking a dissonant note that heralds the passing of Gothic.

CHAPTER 22

MINIMAL GOTHIC AND THE FIELD HOUSE

T hree drawings made for the Field House between 1924 and 1930 illustrate the growing conflict between the architectural style which the University had followed for nearly forty years and the institution's functional demands.

When, in 1924, Amos Alonzo Stagg announced his program for the development of athletic facilities, the accompanying publicity included a drawing for a field house adjacent to Bartlett Gymnasium and continuous in style. [1] Holabird and Roche, who were working on the city's Grant Park stadium at the time, prepared the drawing for the brochure. The chief requirements for the Field House were that it be: spacious enough to accommodate football, baseball, basketball, and track; high enough to allow for soaring balls; and commodious enough

Drawing for a field house, Holabird and Roche, 1924

Revised drawing for a field house, Holabird and Roche, 1925

to seat 8,000 spectators. It seemed improbable that it could be attached to Bartlett, convenient as that might be, without dwarfing the earlier building.

A second drawing prepared by the architects showed the Field House on the northeast corner of 56th Street and Greenwood Avenue. Although these general plans were approved, Thomas E. Donnelley, not fully satisfied, wrote Martin Ryerson, "The first sketches looked so much like a railway station or an armory that I felt it would be out of keeping with any future development of adjacent property, and suggested to the architects that they give it more of a residential or institutional touch." Donnelley, aware of the conflict between the building's function and the University's desire for architectural conformity, continued, "If this field house were to be standing alone in the field, I would be in favor of a more honest expression of its purpose, but I felt a compromise was desirable."[2]

Revised sketches were approved with suggestions that the side parapet be raised, the parapet walls at each end of the south wall be made into gables, and the oriel windows be depressed to keep within property lines.[3] Holabird planned to take bids for both gray and red brick.[4] A committee was appointed to decide the content of the ornamentation.[5]

When bids were taken they were so far over budget that the architects were asked to redraw the plans. In the resulting sketch the building, now of limestone, was reoriented so that it ran east and west, fronting on University Avenue, its silhouette made as plain and crisp as possible, with a peaked roof running the entire length of the building and providing one huge gable at each end. The interest of the building derived from the long lancet windows puncturing the facade and the flat shallow buttresses. All ornamentation and superficial indications of a Gothic allegiance were eliminated.

This simple building was accepted without any of the doubts raised earlier by Donnelley. The *University of Chicago Magazine* described it as a "striking structure, imposing in its mass and in the sweep of its great arena. The design is Gothic, the exterior is limestone and the roof is red tile, so that the building harmonizes rather successfully with the rest of the University."[6] Even though the earlier version with its lavish detail had been widely pub-

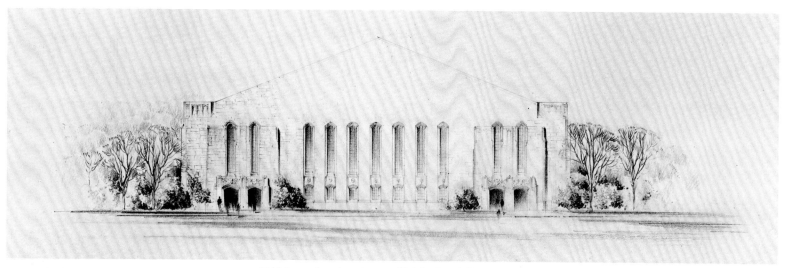

Field house facade redrawn, Holabird and Root, 1930

licized only five years previously, there was apparently no feeling that it would have been preferable or more appropriate.

Voices of modernism were beginning to be heard on campus. George C. Nimmons, a well-known Chicago architect, praised the University, noting, "there is probably no institution which has as large and complete units done in one harmonious style of architecture and with one kind of building material as right here in Chicago." But, he went on to say, "I believe there is no question but that we have finally arrived at a time when there will be a decided change in the architectural treatment of American buildings. . . . In fact the change has already begun. . . . there is scarcely a prominent architect now in this country who will continue . . . to conform nearly as much to conventional lines as formerly. . . . the public has reached a point where it desires change. It seems to have become tired of the old work and to want something new."[7]

In its ready acceptance of the Field House, the University community corroborated Nimmons's statement.

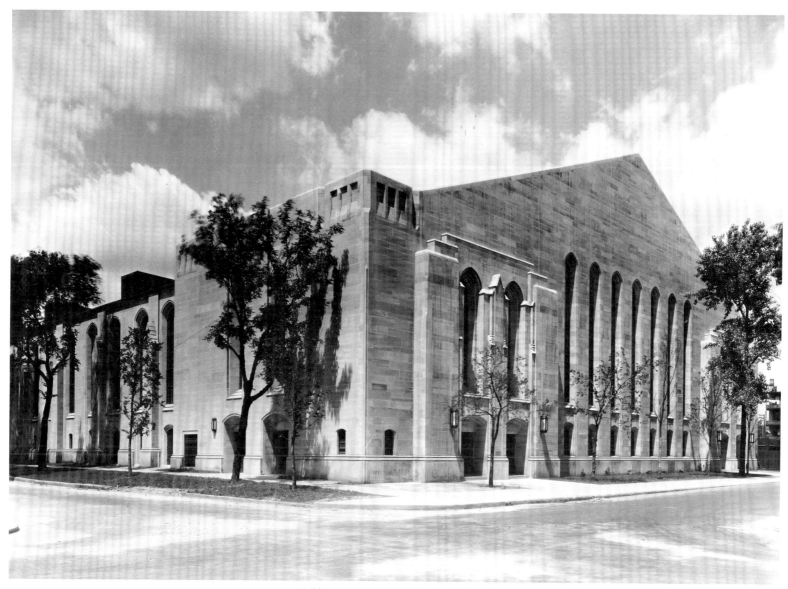

Field House, Holabird and Root, 1932

A CENTURY OF PROGRESS
AND THE DEMISE OF GOTHIC

As the last of the buildings envisioned in Burton's program were being dedicated, a second Chicago world's fair, A Century of Progress, was being hammered and riveted into place on the lake front four miles north of the University. John Holabird, whose firm was building International House and the Field House, was a member of the planning board for A Century of Progress and architect for several of its buildings, including the Chrysler Building. During the summer of 1933 the University was the scene of numerous scholarly conferences. As many as 5,000 visitors a day toured the campus, viewing the glories of Rockefeller Chapel with its organ and carillon, the Oriental Institute, and International House.

Chrysler Building, A Century of Progress, *Holabird and Root, 1933*

Oriental Institute poster inviting fair visitors to the University, 1933

Both the World's Columbian Exposition and A Century of Progress were fantasy lands designed to amuse and instruct, but there were important differences in their scope and emphasis. Architecturally, the 1893 fair was deeply rooted in the past. A Century of Progress took as its central theme the growth of science and its application to industry and the arts of life. Its architecture was described as "modernistic," or "futuristic," expressing the machine age. It was characterized by geometric forms, flat surfaces, sparse ornamentation, and the use of new materials and methods of construction. Professor Robert Morss Lovett, who had come to teach at the University in 1893, summarized the difference between the two fairs: "No greater contrast can be imagined than that between the chaste, classical architectural forms, white as Greek statues, of

the Fair of 1893, and the violently cubistic structures in the motley colors of the clown which were their successors. The contrast is significant of a change in civilization. . . . Technology has replaced culture as the motive of the present century."[1]

In the University, this was also a period of fresh beginnings. Under President Hutchins the administrative and academic structure of the University had been completely reorganized and was being widely publicized.[2] A break with the past was marked by the cessation of University publications that had appeared regularly for the past forty years: the *President's Report*, the *University Register*, and the *University Record*. The *University Record*, in particular, had recounted the past and enriched the University's sense of the weight and purpose of its own tradition.

There were, furthermore, changes in the way the building program was regarded. The belief, so often expressed in the early years, that the University's buildings, like those of Oxford and Cambridge, would endure for hundreds of years, was no longer prevalent. It had been severely challenged by the

rapidity with which the first science buildings and Harper Library had become inadequate. A twelve-volume University survey published in 1933 listed the factors affecting the costs of educational buildings of an institution of higher learning, including degree of permanency, materials employed, amount of ornamentation, and type of interior finish.[3] Its recommendation concerning the building program, though tactfully couched, was in essence a rejection of what had been done in the past. "Buildings erected forty years ago, which were planned in the light of the best available standards of that time, are now educationally obsolete and possibly a real, though oftentimes unrealized handicap in the instructional process. Furthermore, the University has invested large funds in its plant; these funds might have been educationally more productive if applied to endowment and used as a source of support for the current program. These two considerations—the rapid obsolescence of educational buildings and the relatively greater need for endowment—lead to the suggestion that in the future it be the policy to employ a somewhat cheaper type of construction."[4]

People were looking at the campus with different eyes. Parts of it were beginning to appear old-

Robert Maynard Hutchins, President and Chancellor of the University,
1929–1951

fashioned. There were plans to tear down Foster Hall and Haskell Oriental Museum. [5] The Midway entrance of the President's House was remodeled, the porch removed to make the exterior look less heavy and allow more light to reach the drawing room. At President and Mrs. Hutchins's request the doorway was made "less ornate."[6] There was a suggestion that the spire of Kent Laboratory be changed. [7]

Hutchins's reorganization extended to the Board of Trustees, which eliminated its Committee on Buildings and Grounds. The last meeting was held on March 21, 1932. Martin Ryerson died the following August. The next spring A Century of Progress opened.

When the University resumed building after World War II, the designs would be in a contemporary style. The day of architectural historicism had passed, both in the city and on the campus, and Gothic could no longer fulfill the needs and aspirations of the University. [8]

APPENDICES

LANDSCAPING BY OLMSTED BROTHERS

In May 1902, the trustees engaged John C. Olmsted to prepare a landscape plan for the University. As President Harper remarked, "In the earlier days, when buildings were being erected on every side, and tunnels for heat and light were being constructed, it did not seem worth while to take up the consideration of grounds."[1] By the turn of the century it was apparent that something had to be done. Wooden sidewalks and meandering footpaths laced the campus. Building excavations had left their scars. The Trustees' Committee on Buildings and Grounds wanted trees, and Ossian C. Simonds was engaged to plant vines, trees, shrubbery, and lawns.[2]

Simonds's plan was similar to the one he had used in designing Graceland Cemetery: an informal park

Aerial view of the campus, 1901

Botany Pond, ca. 1904

with curving roads and walks, irregular beds and shrubs, and undulating lawns. Neither the faculty nor the trustees were pleased with Simonds's work, and Charles Hutchinson took the initiative in asking John C. Olmsted to visit the campus and consult with Simonds. The Olmsted firm had worked with Shepley, Rutan and Coolidge in creating the campus for Stanford University in the late eighties. They were also well-known in Chicago for having laid out the grounds and lagoons for the World's Columbian Exposition in 1893.[3]

Olmsted visited the campus twice in late 1901, recording his impressions in his journal.[4] In March 1902, he submitted a 36-page comprehensive report to the trustees. He found the Simonds approach both inadequate and unsuitable. He emphasized that in planning it was important to work with the faculty, trustees, and architects, not only in regard to existing buildings but in anticipating future construction, pointing out that, "Through the failure to pursue such a course is due the sad lack of system and harmony in the location and arrangement of most of our most important universities." He felt that Simonds's plan was quite out of harmony with the requirements of the cam-

pus, because "the buildings are many times more important than the grounds and . . . their layout and massive imposing architectural style absolutely demand, from an artistic point of view, a corresponding simplicity, formality, and dignity in the treatment of the grounds."

Instead of starting with the planting, as Simonds had done, he suggested laying out a system of walks and drives, in cooperation with the architect, which would provide for the movement of supplies and wastes as well as people. Keeping in mind the block plan of the quadrangles, he suggested that these walks and drives be laid out on the simplest possible geometric system, with axial vistas at either end. Planting should aim for broad natural landscape effects rather than an emphasis on individual trees and shrubs. He suggested that large American elms be planted and added that "the comparative simplicity of some of the buildings, not to say the slight suggestion of clumsiness, seems to make it desirable to train vines upon the buildings."[5]

The trustees had asked Simonds to prettify the campus. Olmsted showed them what would be necessary to organize it into a coherent whole. His

Hutchinson Court, dedication of the Alice Freeman Palmer Chimes, 1908

Hitchcock Court, ca. 1903

F.1550

Central quadrangle, ca. 1916

report favoring a formal rather than a park treatment was approved and resulted in the Olmsted Brothers being employed by the University. During the ensuing years the firm prepared plans for four courts, the central quadrangle, and Yerkes Observatory. [6]

The court for Hull Biological Laboratories was designed in collaboration with Professor John M. Coulter of the botany department. Its most important feature was a small pond. The pond was lined in concrete which extended six inches above the surface of the water, the earth coming up to its edge, so that it would not show as curbing. The borders were planted with water plants and waterside shrubbery. [7]

Hutchinson Court was conceived as an outdoor congregating space. A sunken garden was ringed by a simple rectangular drive and criss-crossed by diagonal walks. A single row of trees was planted around the edge. It was ready in time for the dedication of the Alice Freeman Palmer Chimes in Mitchell Tower in 1908. In 1914 a fountain, given by Charles Hutchinson, was installed as an architectural centerpiece.

Hitchcock Court received a similar treatment: a sunken, sodded garden with diagonal paths, surrounded by a rectangular driveway. Harper Court was also rectilinear, and a system of clean-cut walkways and clearly differentiated drives provided ready access to all of the buildings in the central quadrangle. Care was taken in planting the trees so as not to obscure axial vistas or to block daylight from buildings.

Olmsted's respect for the interrelationships between the buildings and the landscape; his ability to work with faculty, trustees, and architects; his methodical and practical approach; and his feeling for the most direct and simple, yet visually pleasing scheme for landscape planning and planting resulted in arrangements which are still essentially intact today.

LANDSCAPING BY BENNETT, PARSONS & FROST AND BEATRIX FARRAND

The building program of the twenties demanded renewed landscaping efforts. Not only was it aesthetically desirable to landscape around the new buildings, but the surface of the entire campus would have to be reconstituted after the installation of the heating tunnels connecting each of the buildings with the new Blackstone Avenue Power Plant on 60th Street. The old lamp posts, some of them inherited from the time of the World's Columbian Exposition, were wearing out,[1] and exterior lighting was required for new buildings. Problems of developing an effective and pleasing landscape design were further complicated by the increase in automobile traffic and its attendant nuisances and hazards, which had not been anticipated in the Olmsted plans. Nor had the first Trustees' Committee on Buildings and Grounds been

NO. 0-9217 DATE June 19-1929
U. of C. North tunnel extension, Area No. 15, Looking E.
Engineers Neiler, Rich & Co.
CONTRACTOR Jacobson Bros.

East-west utility tunnel excavation, 1929

Hospital court, Bennett, Parsons & Frost, 1927

able to foresee that locating the main entrances to the buildings on the quadrangles rather than on the street would result in heavy automobile and truck use within what had been planned as a cloistered retreat.

On the recommendation of Thomas E. Donnelley and Martin A. Ryerson the architectural consulting firm of Bennett, Parsons & Frost was asked to study the quadrangles, the medical center, and the location of lamp posts and sidewalks. [2] Edward H. Bennett had been a leader in city planning in Chicago, having worked with Daniel Burnham from 1903 until Burnham's death in 1919, notably on the 1909 Chicago Plan, and in other cities as well. [3] After Burnham died, Bennett established his own private practice devoted to planning. With John Holabird and Hubert Burnham, he was an architectural commissioner for A Century of Progress, and in collaboration with them designed some of its most impressive buildings. [4] The engagement of this firm underscored the continuing commitment of the trustees to comprehensive and long-range planning.

While Bennett, Parsons & Frost worked out the general outlines of their plans, Root and Hollister, landscape architects, assisted in the selection of plants. The chief contributions of Bennett, Parsons & Frost were the plan for the fore-court of Billings Hospital, [5] the interior hospital court, [6] the divinity quadrangle with its flagstone walks, trees, and shrubs, [7] and the landscaping of Rockefeller Chapel. [8] They were also consulted regarding the closing of the east-west drive south of Jones and Kent Laboratories, the drive on the east side between Cobb Hall and the Classics Building, and the development of the grounds for the women's quadrangle, with the consequent closing of its access drive. [9] During this period these driveways were replaced by flagstone walks or grassed over, the time being particularly auspicious because of the repairs necessitated by the tunnel excavations.

At the end of 1929, Emery Jackson recommended that the University retain Beatrix Farrand as an adviser on planning and planting. [10] She had been landscape consultant for Princeton for seventeen years and adviser on planting for the Harkness quadrangles at Yale. Jackson suggested that Mrs. Farrand be consulted on a general campus plan and detailed landscaping for Sunny Gymnasium. One

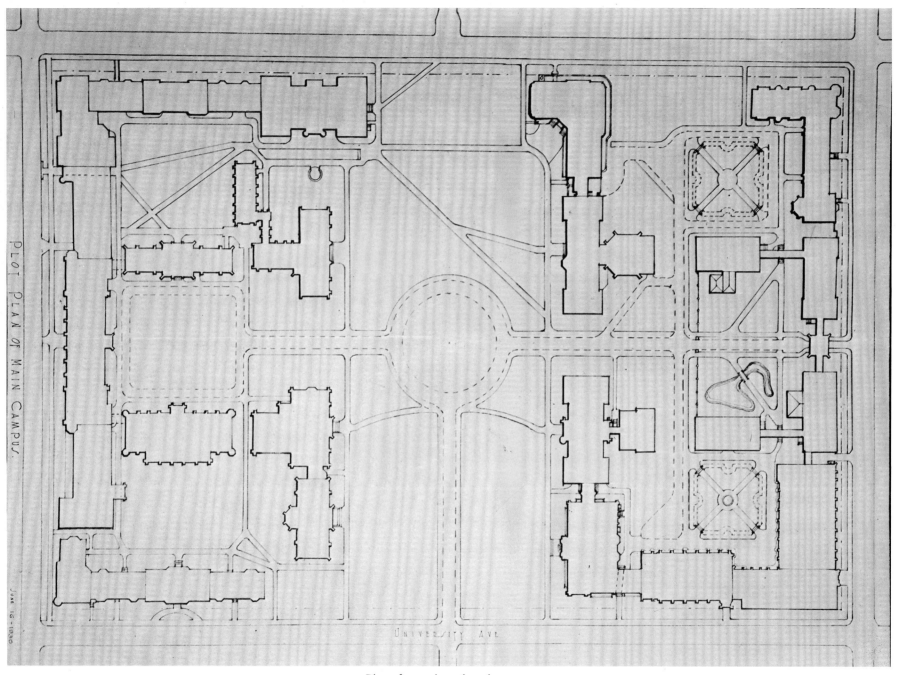

Plan of central quadrangle, 1930

204 APPENDICES

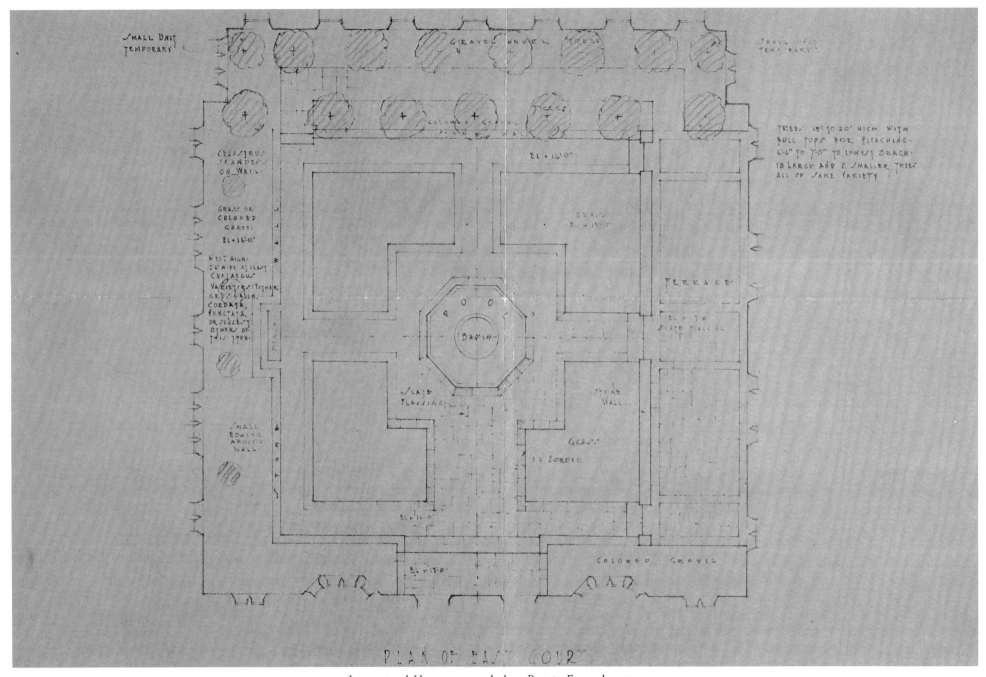

International House courtyard plan, Beatrix Farrand, 1931

of her first contributions was a carload of forsythia she obtained as a gift from Yale, where she had been instrumental in establishing a nursery.[11] The forsythia was planted around Jackman Field[12] just east of Sunny Gymnasium.

Early in 1930 she was given a ground plan of the central quadrangles and asked to make landscape suggestions for separate quadrangles and treatments around recently completed buildings. During this period Mrs. Farrand saw to completion her landscape plans for the Oriental Institute, International House, Eckhart Hall, and Burton-Judson Courts.[13]

Her most important effort, however, the revision of walks and drives on the main campus, never came to fruition. After studying the ground plan, Mrs. Farrand suggested in her report "the acceptance of the general principle that roads be gradually reduced to the minimum necessary for actual service and that walks be placed on actual traffic lanes as nearly as may be consistent with good design."[14] She envisioned that all drives would eventually be removed from campus with the exception of a service drive from Ellis Avenue to the chemical laboratories and a driveway off University Avenue to Mandel Hall. The circle and drives on the axes of

Burton-Judson Courts landscaping, Beatrix Farrand, 1932

the campus were to be taken out and replaced by walks. Some of the walks were to be so built that they could be used as drives on special occasions, making possible an approach by automobile to Bond Chapel and access to the campus buildings by fire apparatus. The main quadrangle was to be planted with a double row of trees on the north and south sides, with clumps of trees on the sides and ends.

The report and plan were approved by the Trustees' Committee on Buildings and Grounds,[15] but implementing the plan was not economically feasible during the thirties, though it remained an objective for the future.[16]

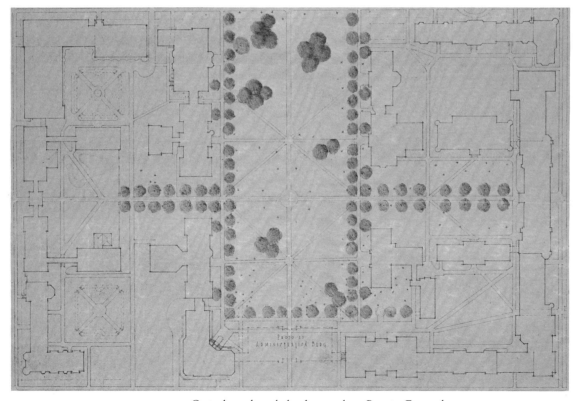

Central quadrangle landscape plan, Beatrix Farrand, 1932

BUILDINGS IN BRICK

Although the campus derived its feeling of unity from the predominant use of Bedford limestone, brick was used for peripheral buildings for reasons both of economy and suitability. Limestone was considered formal, brick informal.

The first of these buildings, the President's House (1895), of pale Roman brick with limestone trim, was a simple though commodious structure linked by its sharply peaked roof and dormers, as well as small touches of Gothic detailing, to its neighbor across the street, Foster Hall. The decision to use brick instead of stone was apparently the architect's and made for reasons of economy. [1]

The first Quadrangle Club (1896), on the corner

President's House, Henry Ives Cobb, 1895

First Quadrangle Club (now Ingleside Hall), Charles B. Atwood, 1896

Lexington Hall (demolished 1981), James Gamble Rogers, 1903

of University Avenue and 58th Street, was designed by Charles B. Atwood, who had also been the architect for the Fine Arts Building at the 1893 Exposition, now the Museum of Science and Industry. The Club had the appearance of an English country house with a few neo-classical features. In 1929 the building was moved to 58th and Ingleside to clear space for the Chapel Block. [2] To the south was Lexington Hall, the temporary building for

women, designed by James Gamble Rogers in 1902 and demolished in 1981. Its sole decorative features, the pedimented columned entrances, relate it to Atwood's building.

As planning progressed for the Press Building, Professor William Gardner Hale expressed a concern for its architectural style in a letter to Harper. "Though simple, it should be in evident relation to

University Press Building, Shepley, Rutan and Coolidge, 1902

Power Plant (demolished 1983), A.D. Houghton, 1902

the University buildings (that is, be essentially of the Gothic order rather than that of the Classical)."[3] Cobb's preliminary plans for the Press Building were said to embody some of the features of Queen's College, Cambridge.[4] Presumably this meant it would be red brick. When Shepley, Rutan and Coolidge took over the project, the firm designed a building which fit in with its Gothic surroundings without in any way imitating them. The building's apparent division into three sections is reminiscent of a row of shops in an English town; its arched first-floor windows suggest a colonnade traditionally associated with a marketplace. Behind the Press Building and erected at the same time was the Power Plant, also of brick and designed in utter simplicity by John D. Rockefeller's engineer, A. D. Houghton.

In time, Ellis Avenue was lined by brick buildings. Ellis Hall, originally erected to house the Labora-

Whitman Laboratory, Coolidge and Hodgdon, 1926

Quadrangle Club, Howard Van Doren Shaw, 1922

tory School, later provided space for the Law School before finally becoming a book store. Ricketts Laboratory North and Ricketts Laboratory South, both long one-story brick structures, provided needed space for animal laboratories. They were, in the twenties, augmented by Whitman Laboratory, also of brick, with a few Classical features that linked it to the Press Building.

Howard Van Doren Shaw, who had built a number of Tudor houses for faculty on adjoining streets,

was architect for the new Quadrangle Club, completed in 1922. [5] Like Cobb, he wanted his design to recall Cambridge. "The Quadrangle Club is a free treatment of Domestic Gothic carried out in red brick like many of the colleges of Cambridge. By the use of this style and color note, the building is designed as a foil to the continuous grayness of the 'Collegiate Gothic' of the University, where, because of the sameness of color, the various buildings are in danger of losing their individuality."[6]

METHODS OF CONSTRUCTION

At the time the University was founded, steel-framed skyscrapers had been rising in downtown Chicago for several years, but this kind of construction was not considered necessary or appropriate for educational institutions. The University owned ample tracts of land and there was no need for buildings to reach great heights. Thus, Cobb, though well known in Chicago as one of the city's first architects to develop methods for constructing fireproof buildings, designed his early structures, including Cobb Hall, the men's and women's residences, and Ryerson and Kent laboratories, using ordinary wooden joists. [1]

Records for this period are scanty; the earliest detailed set of specifications to survive is for the superstructure of the Tower Group, built of brick

Cobb Hall under construction, 1892

faced with stone supported by steel beams and girders. [2]

The first University buildings using reinforced concrete were those for the School of Education, Blaine and Belfield Halls, described by their architect, James Gamble Rogers, as "absolutely fireproof." The flooring in Blaine consisted of twelve cement slabs, each 25 by 88 feet. [3]

The use of reinforced concrete rather than structural steel and terra cotta fireproofing for Harper Library provided a considerable saving and was recommended by Shepley, Rutan and Coolidge as being an entirely satisfactory method. [4] After the disastrous collapse of the west tower on March 29, 1911, however, the trustees voted to rebuild it with a steel frame. [5]

Rockefeller Chapel is the only building on the campus constructed in an essentially medieval manner. The buttressed walls are stone, backed by brick, and finished on the interior with cement. Their enormous weight necessitates a broad base. The bottoms of the tower walls are over eight feet thick and the foundations go down to bedrock eighty

The brick backing to be bonded in with the stone ashler as required.

BRICK TO BE WET:

All brick used in the buildings shall be good, hard, well-burned brick, and if used during the months from March to December inclusive, shall be well wet at the time they are used.

ANCHORING:

In no case shall one wall be carried up more than fifteen (15) feet in advance of other walls.

The interior and exterior walls will be anchored to every steel beam with wrought iron anchors of the size called for by the specifications.

The ends of the roof trusses and the ends of the steel girders shall be securely anchored to the walls as directed.

The stone facing on plain walls will be anchored to the brick backing with tarred wrought iron anchors to be one and one-quarter (1-1/4") inches wide by three-sixteenths (3/16") of an inch thick, and of the length required by the different thicknesses of the walls. There will be one anchor for every stone three feet long or under; and two anchors for every stone over three feet long.

Set in the walls the necessary anchors for anchoring the expanded metal and concrete floors at levels shown.

Build in all other rods, bolts, tie-beams and anchors shown and required for the anchoring of the bay windows to main walls, and the stone facing to the brick backings and iron framework.

Set in place any other anchoring that may be required.

-12-

Tower Group specifications, Shepley, Rutan and Coolidge, 1901

JULY,5-1910
B.7127

Harper Library under construction, 1910

Harper Library, collapse of west tower, March 11, 1911

feet below the floor level. The only structural steel is in the vertical supports and floor of the tower, the undergirding for the choir and organ lofts, and the roof trusses. Lyman Flook, superintendent of buildings and grounds, instituted a careful system of record-keeping involving daily reports and monthly photographs which offer a documented history of the University's building projects during the late twenties. From these records it is possible to study the entire construction process of Rockefeller Chapel.

The desirability of constructing buildings with load-bearing walls was being questioned in the late twenties. Flook put the matter to Lloyd Steere, the University's business manager: "I think we should give serious consideration to the design of the structure of the Orthopedics Hospital to see if we cannot design it as a concrete frame and curtain-wall building instead of a wall-bearing building such as Social Science and Bobs Roberts . . . and for this project make as good time as for Bernard Edward Sunny Gymnasium. The architects have always used the argument in favor of the wall-bearing building that they needed the thickness . . . in order to get the deep reveals necessary in Gothic design."[6] Concrete frame and curtain-wall construction greatly increased the speed with which a building could be erected. The photographs of Sunny Gymnasium illustrate this method.

Although the trustees voted not to use the newer method of construction for the orthopedics hospital, it was inevitable that the University adopt it for future buildings. Burton-Judson Courts and International House, because of their great size, were obvious candidates for the new way of building, their concrete frames and steel girders being sheathed by a thin masonry skin.

University Chapel under construction, June 1, 1927

Sunny Gymnasium under construction, 1929

Burton-Judson Courts under construction, 1931

CHRONOLOGICAL BUILDING LIST 1892-1932

Name	Date Completed	Donor	Architect
Cobb Lecture Hall	1892	Silas B. Cobb	Henry Ives Cobb
Blake Hall	1892	John D. Rockefeller and others	Henry Ives Cobb
Gates Hall	1892	John D. Rockefeller and others	Henry Ives Cobb
Goodspeed Hall	1892	John D. Rockefeller and others	Henry Ives Cobb
Temporary Gymnasium and Library (demolished 1903)	1892	General University funds	
Beecher Hall	1893	Mrs. Jerome Beecher	Henry Ives Cobb
Kelly Hall	1893	Mrs. Elizabeth G. Kelly	Henry Ives Cobb
Foster Hall	1893	Mrs. Nancy Foster	Henry Ives Cobb
Snell Hall	1893	Mrs. Henrietta Snell	Henry Ives Cobb
Walker Museum	1893	George C. Walker	Henry Ives Cobb
Ryerson Physical Laboratory	1894	Martin A. Ryerson	Henry Ives Cobb
Kent Chemical Laboratory	1894	Sidney A. Kent	Henry Ives Cobb
President's House	1895	General University funds	Henry Ives Cobb
Quadrangle Club (now Ingleside Hall)	1896	Quadrangle Club members	Charles B. Atwood

Haskell Oriental Museum (now Haskell Hall)	1896	Mrs. Caroline Haskell	Henry Ives Cobb
Hull Biological Laboratories	1897	Miss Helen Culver	Henry Ives Cobb
Anatomy			
Botany (now Ida B. and Walter Erman Biology Center)			
Physiology (now Culver Hall)			
Zoology			
Yerkes Observatory	1897	Charles T. Yerkes	Henry Ives Cobb
Green Hall	1899	Mrs. Elizabeth G. Kelly	Henry Ives Cobb
Ellis Hall (demolished 1970)	1901	General University funds	Shepley, Rutan and Coolidge
Hitchcock Hall	1902	Mrs. Charles Hitchcock	Dwight Heald Perkins
Power Plant (later Service Building) (demolished 1983)	1902	John D. Rockefeller	A. D. Houghton
University Press (now Book Store)	1902	John D. Rockefeller	Shepley, Rutan and Coolidge
School of Education Temporary Gymnasium (demolished 1959)	1902	General University funds	James Gamble Rogers
Hutchinson Commons	1903	Charles L. Hutchinson	Shepley, Rutan and Coolidge
Reynolds Club	1903	Mrs. Joseph Reynolds	Shepley, Rutan and Coolidge
Mandel Hall	1903	Leon Mandel	Shepley, Rutan and Coolidge
Mitchell Tower	1903	John J. Mitchell	Shepley, Rutan and Coolidge
Lexington Hall (demolished 1981)	1903	General University funds	James Gamble Rogers
Blaine Hall	1903	Mrs. Emmons Blaine	James Gamble Rogers
Belfield Hall	1904	John D. Rockefeller and sale of property of Chicago Manual Training School	James Gamble Rogers

Bartlett Gymnasium	1904	Adolphus C. Bartlett	Shepley, Rutan and Coolidge
Law School (now Stuart Hall)	1904	John D. Rockefeller and others	Shepley, Rutan and Coolidge
Harper Memorial Library	1912	John D. Rockefeller and Harper Memorial Fund	Shepley, Rutan and Coolidge
Stagg Field (demolished 1965)	1913	General University funds	Shepley, Rutan and Coolidge
Ryerson Physical Laboratory Annex	1913	Martin A. Ryerson	Shepley, Rutan and Coolidge
Ricketts Laboratory North (demolished 1983)	1914	General University funds	Holabird and Roche
Classics Building—Hiram Kelly Memorial	1915	Mrs. Elizabeth G. Kelly	Shepley, Rutan and Coolidge
Rosenwald Hall	1915	Julius Rosenwald	Holabird and Roche
Ida Noyes Hall	1916	La Verne Noyes	Shepley, Rutan and Coolidge
Quadrangle Club	1922	Quadrangle Club members and general University funds	Howard Van Doren Shaw
Ricketts Laboratory South (demolished 1966)	1922	General University funds	Henry K. Holsman
Swift Hall	1926	Mrs. Gustavus Swift	Coolidge and Hodgdon
Bond Chapel	1926	Mrs. Joseph Bond	Coolidge and Hodgdon
Whitman Laboratory	1926	Mr. and Mrs. Frank Lillie	Coolidge and Hodgdon
University Clinics	1927	General Education Board and private donors	Coolidge and Hodgdon
Physiology Building (now Abbott Hall)	1927	General Education Board and private donors	Coolidge and Hodgdon
University Chapel (now Rockefeller Chapel)	1928	John D. Rockefeller	Bertram Grosvenor Goodhue; completed by Goodhue Associates: Mayers, Murray and Phillip

Wieboldt Hall	1928	Wieboldt Foundation	Coolidge and Hodgdon
Social Science Research Building	1929	Laura Spelman Rockefeller Memorial Fund	Coolidge and Hodgdon
Jones Laboratory	1929	George Herbert Jones	Coolidge and Hodgdon
Sunny Gymnasium	1929	Bernard E. Sunny	Armstrong, Furst and Tilton
Blackstone Avenue Power Plant	1929	General University funds	Neiler, Rich, Engineers; Philip Maher, Consulting Architect
Bobs Roberts Memorial Hospital	1930	Bobs Roberts Memorial Hospital for Children Corporation	Coolidge and Hodgdon
Eckhart Hall	1930	Bernard A. Eckhart	Charles Z. Klauder
Barnes Laboratory	1930	General Education Board	Perkins, Chatten and Hammond
Judd Hall	1931	General Education Board	Armstrong, Furst and Tilton
Burton-Judson Courts	1931	Julius Rosenwald	Zantzinger, Borie and Medary
Oriental Institute	1931	General Education Board	Mayers, Murray and Phillip, formerly Goodhue Associates
Chicago Lying-in Hospital	1931	Chicago Lying-in Hospital	Schmidt, Garden and Erikson
Hicks-McElwee Orthopedic Hospital	1931	Gertrude Dunn Hicks, Elizabeth Spalding McElwee, through the Home for Destitute Crippled Children	Coolidge and Hodgdon
International House	1932	John D. Rockefeller, Jr.	Holabird and Root
Field House (now Henry Crown Field House)	1932	Receipts from athletic department events	Holabird and Root

NOTES

ABBREVIATIONS

The following abbreviations refer to manuscripts, records, and record series in the University of Chicago Archives. Additional manuscript materials cited in the notes are also in the Archives unless otherwise indicated.

ABF	Archival Biographical Files
ABg	Archival Building Files
BG	Department of Buildings and Grounds Records
BT	Minutes of the Board of Trustees
CBT	Correspondence of the Board of Trustees
CF	Correspondence of the Founder and His Associates
EDB	Ernest DeWitt Burton Papers
EJG	Edgar J. Goodspeed Papers
GCW	George C. Walker Papers
HHS	Harold H. Swift Papers
MT	Marion Talbot Papers
OG	*University of Chicago Official Guides, 1916, 1918, 1921, 1923, 1928, 1930*
PP	Presidents' Papers, 1889–1925
PR	*President's Report, 1892–1930*
QC	*Quarterly Calendar, 1892–96*
RDS	Rollin D. Salisbury Papers
TBG	Minutes of the Trustees' Committee on Buildings and Grounds
TCC	Thomas C. Chamberlin Papers
UCB	Thomas W. Goodspeed, *The University of Chicago Biographical Sketches*, 2 vols. (Chicago: University of Chicago Press, 1925)
UCM	*University of Chicago Magazine, 1907–*
UCW	*University of Chicago Weekly, 1892–1901*
UR	*University Record, 1896–1933*
URg	*Annual Register of the University of Chicago, 1892–1930*
WRH	William Rainey Harper Papers

NOTES

PROLOGUE: THE GRAY CITY AND THE WHITE CITY

1. William Rainey Harper to Charles L. Hutchinson, Mar. 25, 1891, and Hutchinson to Harper, Mar. 21, 1891, PP 65:11; Elmer L. Corthell to Harper, Nov. 25, 1892, CBT 1:2.

2. Cobb was appointed to the National Board of Architects for the Exposition on Jan. 10, 1891. He was selected as University architect the following June.

3. Thomas W. Goodspeed to Harper, Dec. 10, 1890, WRH 9:7. For accounts of the founding and early history of the University see Thomas Wakefield Goodspeed, *A History of the University of Chicago: The First Quarter-Century* (Chicago: University of Chicago Press, 1916) and Richard J. Storr, *Harper's University: The Beginnings* (Chicago: University of Chicago Press, 1966).

4. Cobb's work at the Exposition is dealt with by Montgomery Schuyler in "A Critique of the Works of Adler and Sullivan, D. H. Burnham and Co., Henry Ives Cobb," *Architectural Record, Great American Architects Series*, No. 2, Dec. 1895, and Henry Van Brunt, *Architecture and Society, Selected Essays*, ed. William A. Coles (Cambridge, Mass.: The Belknap Press of Harvard University Press, 1969).

5. *The Standard*, July 6, 1893, GCW 1:7.

6. Edwin Herbert Lewis (1866–1938) wrote "Alma Mater" while a graduate student. He received his Ph.D. in 1894. See Edwin Herbert Lewis, *University of Chicago Poems* (Chicago: University of Chicago Press, 1923).

7. William Rainey Harper (1856–1906), President of the University and Head Professor of Semitic Languages and Literature, received his A.B. from Muskingum College in 1870, his Ph.D. from Yale University in 1875. He had been principal of Denison University, 1879–80, professor of Hebrew and cognate languages at Baptist Union Theological Seminary, 1879–86, and principal of the Chautauqua College of Liberal Arts, 1885–91. When he accepted the presidency of the University he was principal of the Chautauqua System and of the American Institute of Sacred Literature, and Woolsey Professor of Biblical Literature at Yale. For a biography of Harper see Thomas Wakefield Goodspeed, *William Rainey Harper, First President of the University of Chicago* (Chicago: University of Chicago Press, 1928).

8. William Rainey Harper, *The Trend in Higher Education* (Chicago: University of Chicago Press, 1905), pp. 23–24.

CHAPTER 1. THE TRUSTEES' COMMITTEE ON BUILDINGS AND GROUNDS

1. The other members were Andrew MacLeish, Francis E. Hinckley, Henry A. Rust, George C. Walker, Elmer Corthell, and Eli B. Felsenthal. Their qualifications included leadership in the business community, building and engineering expertise, connections with the Old University of Chicago, fund-raising activity, involvement in Baptist affairs, and participation in shaping Chicago's cultural life.

At the time the committee was appointed, George C. Walker was a grain and provisions merchant and real estate developer; Andrew MacLeish was the founder and manager of Carson, Pirie, Scott and Co.; Charles L. Hutchinson was president of the Corn Exchange Bank, of which Martin Ryerson was a director; Henry Rust was a builder of railways and bridges; and Elmer Corthell, a civil engineer, was construction superintendent of the Mississippi jetties.

Walker and MacLeish had been trustees of the Old University, and Felsenthal, a lawyer, was a graduate.

Hinckley had contributed the first $50,000 to the new institution after John D. Rockefeller's initial gift of $600,000; Felsenthal led the movement which resulted in aid to the University

The First Board of Trustees.

1. President William Rainey Harper
2. E. Nelson Blake
3. Martin A. Ryerson
4. Charles L. Hutchinson
5. George A. Pillsbury
6. Ferd. W. Peck
7. Herman H. Kohlsaat
8. Edward Goodman
9. Alonzo K. Parker
10. John W. Midgley
11. Henry A. Rust
12. George C. Walker
13. C. C. Bowen
14. Andrew McLeish
15. Judge J. W. Bailey
16. Eli B. Fesenthal
17. Judge D. L. Shorey
18. Fred A. Smith
19. Frances E. Hinckley.
20. Elmer L. Corthell
21. W. B. Brayton

The first Board of Trustees

from Chicago's Jewish community; and Hutchinson and Ryerson had not only contributed generously but taken the lead in raising funds among the city's businessmen.

Walker was a member of the College Committee of the Baptist Education Society, MacLeish a trustee of the Baptist Union Theological Society.

Ryerson and Hutchinson were directors of the World's Columbian Exposition and the Chicago Auditorium Association. Hutchinson was president of the Chicago Art Institute and Ryerson a director.

For further biographical material on Hutchinson, Walker, and MacLeish see *UCB*. On Ryerson see *UR*, n. s. VIII, 4, Oct. 1922 and ABF.

Thomas W. Goodspeed (1842–1927) was a Baptist minister and later secretary of the Baptist Union Theological Seminary. It was he who initiated negotiations with Rockefeller to found a Baptist educational institution in Chicago. After the University was chartered he became secretary to the Board of Trustees. Following his retirement he assumed the role of University historian. See Charles Ten Broeke Goodspeed, *Thomas Wakefield Goodspeed* (Chicago: University of Chicago Press, 1932) and *UR*, n. s. XIV, 1, Jan. 1928, pp. 34–39.

2. Goodspeed to Harper, Sept. 7, 1890, CF 1:1. Trinity College had a master plan in the Gothic mode designed by William Burges in 1878. See Richard P. Dober, *Campus Planning* (New York: Reinhold Publishing Co., 1963).

3. Goodspeed to Harper, Oct. 7, 1890, WRH 9:7. Yale's Victorian Gothic buildings dated back to before the Civil War. Those to which Goodspeed was alluding were probably Farnam and Lawrance Halls, designed by Russell Sturgis. See Reuben A. Holden, *Yale: A Pictorial History* (New Haven: Yale University Press, 1967).

4. Goodspeed to Harper, Sept. 21, 1890, WRH 9:7. For Marshall Field see *UCB*, Vol. I.

5. TBG, Jan. 2, 1891.

6. TBG, Apr. 25, 1891.

7. TBG, June 4, 1891. Goodspeed to Harper, June 5, 1891, PP 36:4.

8. GCW 1:5.

9. Goodspeed, *History*, p. 219.

10. GCW 1:5.

11. PP 53:2a.

12. *UCW*, I, 1, Oct. 1, 1892, p. 12.

Silas B. Cobb

CHAPTER 2. A GENERAL RECITATION BUILDING

1. Henry Ives Cobb (1859–1931) was born in Brookline, Massachusetts, attended the Boston public schools, and studied at MIT, after which he traveled in Europe. He came to Chicago in 1881 and remained until 1900, when he opened an office in Washington, and subsequently, in 1902, one in New York. For biographical information see Henry F. Withey and Elsie Rathburn Withey, *Biographical Dictionary of American Artists: Deceased* (Los Angeles: New Age Publishing Co., 1956). Montgomery Schuyler described Cobb's work at the University: "In these refined and enjoyable works the architect has reached a personal expression within the limits of an historical style, and has given evidence of an artistic individuality in addition to the abundant testimony given in his work to a remarkable technical equipment and a really astonishing versatility and facility." Schuyler, "A Critique," Dec. 1895, p. 110. Contemporary descriptions of Cobb's work on the campus include Charles E. Jenkins, "The University of Chicago," *Architectural Record*, 4, 1894; Robert Herrick, "The University of Chicago," *Scribner's Magazine*, Oct. 1895; and *The University of Chicago Weekly Decennial Souvenir 1892–1902*. For a twentieth-century description and analysis see Julius Lewis, "Henry Ives Cobb and the Chicago School" (MA Thesis, University of Chicago, 1954) and Perrin H. Lowrey, "Cobb, the Old: the New," *UCM*, Nov. 1963.

2. Goodspeed to Harper, Oct. 12, 1890, WRH 9:7.

3. "Model Offices—Fourth Series: Description of the Offices of Henry Ives Cobb, Architect," *Inland Architect and News Record* No. 4, May, 1895.

4. See *UCB*, Vol. I.

5. OG, 1916, p. 16.

6. TBG, Dec. 7 and 9, 1891.

7. TBG, July 9 and Sept. 13, 1892.

8. *Inter-Ocean*, Oct. 2, 1892.

CHAPTER 3. A HOUSING SYSTEM FOR MEN

1. Goodspeed to Harper, Sept. 28, 1890, WRH 9:7.

2. Harper to Goodspeed, Oct. 1, 1890, TWG I:4.

3. *Inter-Ocean*, Apr. 21, 1895.

4. *UCW*, May 9, 1895.

Mrs. Henrietta Snell

5. Henrietta Snell to Harper, Jan. 8, 1895, PP 61:6.
6. *PR*, 1892–1902, p. 388.
7. Snell Hall Committee to Goodspeed and trustees, Feb. 15, 1894, CBT 1:6.

CHAPTER 4. A RESIDENTIAL PROGRAM FOR WOMEN
1. Marion Talbot, "Moral and Religious Influences as Related to Environment of Student Life: Dormitory Life for College Women," *Journal of Religious Education Association*, Apr. 1909, MT 7:2.
2. See Edward T. James, Janet Wilson James, and Paul S. Boyer, eds., *Notable American Women 1607–1950: A Biographical Dictionary*, Vol. III (Cambridge, Mass.: The Belknap Press of Harvard University Press, 1971) for biographical material on Alice Freeman

Palmer (1855–1902) and Marion Talbot (1858–1948); also George Herbert Palmer, *The Life of Alice Freeman Palmer* (Boston: Houghton Mifflin Co., 1902); *UR*, XIII, 1, July, 1908, "Dedication of the Alice Freeman Palmer Chimes," pp. 9–17; and ABF for information about both women. Marion Talbot reminisces about her experiences as dean of women, 1892–1925, in *More than Lore* (Chicago: University of Chicago Press, 1936). See also MT.
3. The Wellesley connection was a strong one among the women faculty. Elizabeth Wallace (1868–1961), who became head of Beecher Hall, had graduated from Wellesley in 1886. See Elizabeth Wallace, *The Unending Journey* (Minneapolis: University of Minnesota Press, 1952). Sophonisba Breckinridge (1860–1948), who became Marion Talbot's assistant and house head of Green Hall, and who was later instrumental in forming the School of Social Service Administration, was also a Wellesley graduate.

Mrs. Nancy Foster

Mrs. Jerome Beecher

See ABF and Sophonisba Breckinridge Papers. See also *Notable American Women*, Vol. I.

4. Part of the planning for the women's residences included making arrangements for Ellen H. Richards, first woman faculty member at MIT, to transfer to the University the equipment for the model kitchen she had established at the Columbian Exposition as a means of showing scientific and economical methods of preparing food. Talbot, *More than Lore*, p. 118.

5. Marion Talbot to her parents, Sept. 9, 1892, MT 1:11.

6. *The Graphic*, Apr. 23, 1892, PP 54:2.

7. Cobb to Goodspeed, Jan. 30, 1892, CBT 1:2.

8. *An Appeal on Behalf of Women Students by the Women's Club of Chicago* (Chicago: The University Press of Chicago, 1892). See also "The Women's Building Fund," PP 26:13.

9. TBG, Dec. 3, 1892.

10. Nancy Foster was the wife of Dr. John H. Foster. After her husband's death Mrs. Foster made her home with her daughter and son-in-law, Mr. and Mrs. George Adams, through whom she made her gifts to the University. Mrs. Jerome Beecher was

Mrs. Elizabeth Green Kelly

a sister of Silas Cobb. Beecher Hall is a memorial to her husband, who was one of the earliest Chicagoans to contribute to the fund for the University. Mrs. Elizabeth G. Kelly was the donor of Kelly Hall and Green Hall, named for her parents, and the Classics Building. See OG, 1916. These women donors, and the wives of trustees as well, took a lively interest in furnishing the residences, contributing china, rugs, and furniture. See Marion Talbot to her mother, 1894, MT 1:16; and Alice Freeman Palmer to Harper, Dec. 19, 1893, CBT 1:5.

11. Although the word "gargoyle" is frequently used to describe the protruding chimeras or grotesques on the towers and cornices of University buildings, Calvert W. Audrain, Director of Physical Planning and Construction, has noted that there are very few true gargoyles on campus in the sense that they function as water spouts. Most of the roofs are drained internally.

12. *PR*, 1892–1902, p. 393.

Mrs. Caroline Haskell

CHAPTER 5. MUSEUMS AND PEDAGOGY

1. Walker had been one of the founders and president of the Chicago Academy of Sciences. He wanted the museum to draw from and serve the vast area west of the Alleghenies. As a member of the Trustees' Committee on Buildings and Grounds he was deeply involved in planning for his building.

2. Thomas Chrowder Chamberlin to Rollin D. Salisbury, July 11 and 12, 1892, RDS 4: 1. For the life and work of Chamberlin see Susan F. Schultz, "Thomas C. Chamberlin: An Intellectual Biography of a Geologist and Educator" (Ph. D. Dissertation, University of Wisconsin, 1976) and D. Jerome Fisher, *The Seventy Years of the Department of Geology: University of Chicago 1892–1961* (Chicago: University of Chicago Press, 1963).

3. Cobb to Walker, July 23, 1892, GCW 1: 6.

4. *Inter-Ocean*, Jan. 12, 1893, GCW 1: 7.

5. Chamberlin to Salisbury, July 10, 1893, RDS 3: 18.

6. TBG, Aug. 5, 1893.

7. QC, Nov. 1893, pp. 10–11.

8. Report to Members of the Museum Commission, 1904, TCC 3: 8.

9. Rev. Barrows had organized and led the World Parliament of Religions at the Exposition. For a biography of Frederick Haskell see *UCB*, Vol. II.

10. Harper's cornerstone speech, July 1, 1895, PP 38: 1.

11. QC, Aug. 1895, pp. 27–28.

12. Cobb to Harper, Jan. 7, 1895, PP 7: 8.

13. James Henry Breasted, *The Oriental Institute* (Chicago: University of Chicago Press, 1933) and Charles Breasted, *Pioneer to the Past: The Story of James Henry Breasted, Archaeologist* (New York: Charles Scribner's Sons, 1943).

14. Ira Price Papers, 5, Scrapbook, p. 135.

CHAPTER 6. LABORATORIES FOR THE SCIENCES

1. The University's emphasis on research was considered its outstanding feature. John D. Rockefeller in his *Random Reminiscences of Men and Events* (New York: Doubleday Page and Co., 1909) said, "My interest in the University of Chicago has been enhanced by the fact that while it has comprehensively considered

Yerkes Observatory, Henry Ives Cobb, 1897, Williams Bay, Wisconsin

Sidney A. Kent Memorial Tablet, by Lorado Taft, [n.d.]

Miss Helen Culver

the features of a collegiate course, it has given so much attention to research," p. 177.

Harper constantly reiterated the importance of the sciences. "The thinking of today has to do with what we call science. A century ago there really was no science. The laws of nature were still a secret. . . . The circle of scientific investigation has now, however, gradually extended itself, until it includes everything, from God himself to the most insignificant atom of his creation," Harper, *Trend*, pp. 49–50.

Ryerson, in formally presenting the physical laboratory, took the pragmatic view. "We know that in the presence of the great social and industrial problems of the day we cannot afford to leave concealed any part of the truth which the human is capable of grasping, and that this truth must be sought in the domain of natural science as well as in the domain of religion, ethics, and political science," QC, Aug. 1894, p. 31.

2. Dedicated Jan. 1, 1894, *UCW*, II, 13, p. 9.

3. Opened in Jan., 1894, dedicated July 3, 1894, QC, Aug. 1894.

4. Dedicated July 2, 1897, *UR*, II, 16, p. 149.

5. Dedicated Oct. 21, 1897, *UR*, II, 29, p. 235. Being off-campus, the design of Yerkes Observatory was not subject to the Gothic imperative. Professor of astrophysics George E. Hale was responsible for both the impetus and the planning for the observatory. Finding that there was a 40 inch refracting telescope available, the largest in the world, he persuaded Charles Yerkes to purchase it and mount it for the University, exhibiting it first at the Exposition. It was Hale, also, who brought Cobb and Yerkes together. The observatory was built on Lake Geneva because the Chicago air was too impure to permit accurate observations. Unlike other University buildings, which were subject to review and approval by the trustees, the design and building were entirely in the hands of the donor, the architect, and Hale. After studying the great European observatories, Hale prepared a plan which he sent to Cobb and Harper. Cobb followed it in all its essentials. Hale to Harper, Jan. 1, 1894, PP 37:1. The strict functionalism of the building was stated in Romanesque terms, the arches and columns heavily encrusted with terra cotta ornamentation. In its fine symbolic detailing, as well as its general outline, it is more closely related to Cobb's Fisheries Building for the Exposition than to any structure on the main campus. For the life and work of Hale see Joan N. Warnow and Charles Weiner, eds., *The Legacy of George Ellery Hale* (Cambridge, Mass.: MIT Press, 1972).

6. Sidney Albert Kent (1834–1900) was a Chicago grain speculator and businessman, a member of the Board of Trade and one of the organizers of the Corn Exchange Bank, of which Charles Hutchinson was president. *UCB*, Vol. II.

7. Ryerson's Physical Laboratory, given in memory of his father, a wealthy lumberman and real estate entrepreneur, was one of the earliest building gifts. Ryerson to Board of Trustees, Nov. 1, 1892, PP 65:22.

8. *UCW*, II, 25, p. 1, Apr. 5, 1894.

9. Albert A. Michelson (1852–1931) was head of the Department of Physics from 1894 to 1929. He came to the University from Clark, where he had already achieved an international reputation for his experiments in measuring light. In 1907 he became the first American scientist to receive the Nobel Prize. See Dorothy Livingston, *The Master of Light: A Biography of Albert A. Michelson* (New York: Charles Scribner's Sons, 1973). For an intimate view see Norman F. Maclean, "Billiards is a Good Game," *UCM*, Summer, 1975.

10. BT, Dec. 27, 1895.

11. Helen Culver (1832–1925), pioneer advocate of the vote, education, and business opportunities for women, went into the real estate office of a cousin, Charles J. Hull, a trustee of the Old University, as his assistant. After Hull's death in 1889 she inherited his fortune and became sole head of the firm. In addition to the $1,000,000 she gave for the Hull laboratories, she left the University $600,000 upon her death. *UCB*, Vol. II.

12. Chamberlin to Harper, Nov. 26, 1896, TCC 2:2.

13. Judson to Harper, June 18, 1891, PP 42:11. For a witty denunciation of the University's medieval architecture see Thorstein Veblen, *The Higher Learning in America* (New York: B. W. Huebsch, 1918), pp. 143–47. Veblen was a member of the University faculty from 1892 to 1906.

14. *OG*, 1916, p. 41.

CHAPTER 7. THE END OF THE COBB YEARS

1. Goodspeed to Harper, Oct. 21, 1891, PP 36:4.

2. TBG, May 25, 1892.

3. Hale to Hutchinson, Feb. 5, 1895, PP 65:11.

4. Culver to Harper, Mar. 23, 1897, PP 29:30.

5. Cobb to Goodspeed, June 2, 1900, CBT 1:2.

6. Cobb to Harper, Jan. 23, 1900, PP 7: 8.

7. TBG, May 15, 1901.

CHAPTER 8. OXFORD COMES TO CHICAGO

1. In 1895, Rockefeller contributed $2,000,000 "for endowment or otherwise as I may designate . . . but only in amounts equal to contributions of others." Of this $2,000,000, $1,300,000 went to pay deficits; the rest went for additions to the campus. Goodspeed, *History*, pp. 280–83.

2. Dober, *Campus Planning*, p. 3.

3. Harper wrote Frederick T. Gates, Rockefeller's philanthropic adviser and a trustee of the University, July 29, 1899, "A great deal of trouble is being experienced in renting rooms . . . because of our inability to provide eating facilities close to the University. A great many parents have come and gone away with the feeling that there is no satisfactory provision for young men who are able to pay a reasonable amount of money. I am afraid this feeling is well founded." Cf. Rockefeller Archives Center, Tarrytown, New York. Gymnasium facilities were provided in a temporary building which also housed the Press and the general library.

4. *PR*, 1892–1902, p. xxxiii.

5. *UR*, VI, 13, June 28, 1901.

CHAPTER 9. THE TOWER GROUP

1. George Fisher Shepley (1858–1903), a graduate of Washington University in St. Louis, and Charles Allerton Coolidge (1858–1936), a graduate of Harvard College, both studied architecture at MIT and worked for the Boston firm of Ware and Van Brunt before joining Henry Hobson Richardson's office in 1884. Charles

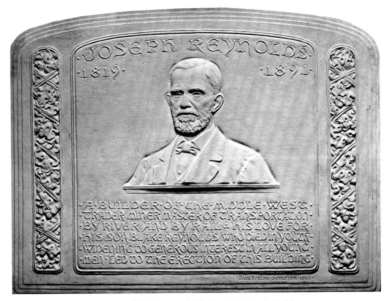

Joseph Reynolds Memorial Tablet, by Paul Fjelde, 1921

Hercules Rutan (1851–1914) went to work for Richardson in 1869 as an office boy, continued as a draftsman, and later became one of the chief designers. After Richardson's death they formed their own firm which completed his work in Chicago for the Marshall Field Warehouse, Glessner House on Prairie Avenue, and the Franklin McVeagh house. When Rutan died, in 1914, the name of the Boston firm was changed to Coolidge and Shattuck. In 1915 a separate partnership was formed with the Chicago manager, Charles Hodgdon. This firm was dissolved in 1930. Working in the Gothic style was the exception rather than the rule for Shepley, Rutan and Coolidge. Its other Chicago buildings were Classically inspired, and its many buildings for Harvard during this period were derived from Georgian prototypes. For a description of the firm in its early days see *Architectural Record, Great*

American Architects, Series 3 July, 1896. See also, J. D. Forbes, "Shepley, Bullfinch, Richardson and Abbott, Architects: An Introduction," *Journal of the Society of Architectural Historians*, XVII, 3, Fall, 1958, and James F. O'Gorman, *H. H. Richardson and His Office* (Cambridge, Mass.: Harvard College Library Department of Printing and Graphic Arts, 1974). For biographical information on Charles Coolidge see *Dictionary of American Biography*, Vol. 22; Harvard College, *Class of 1881, Secretary's Anniversary Reports, 1906, 1921, and 1931; Harvard Alumni Bulletin*, Apr. 10, 1936; and *Architectural Forum*, May 1936.

2. *13th Annual Report of the Board of Trustees of the Chicago Art Institute for the Year 1892.*

3. *Minutes of the Chicago Public Library Board of Directors*, Feb. 27, 1892.

4. The friendship between Coolidge and the Hutchinsons and Ryersons was not only important in shaping the University's building program but resulted in other commissions for Coolidge as well. Between 1892 and 1900 the Coolidges were neighbors of the Hutchinsons on Prairie Avenue. After 1900, when they returned to Boston, Hutchinson's journal (at the Newberry Library) and the Ryersons' guest book for their Lake Geneva summer home (at the Chicago Historical Society) record frequent visits by and dinners with Coolidge. In 1898, the Coolidge firm built the Chicago Orphan Asylum, of which Hutchinson and Ryerson were trustees; in 1902 the Hutchinson's Lake Geneva house, Wychwood; in 1904 the Ryerson Library in Grand Rapids, Michigan; and in 1912 the Corn Exchange Bank, Chicago.

5. *14th Annual Report of the Board of Trustees of the Art Institute*, June, 1893, p. 9.

6. Hutchinson to Harper, Apr. 4, 1900, PP 65:12. Coolidge probably combined this trip with one to Paris where he was United States architect for the Paris Exposition of 1900.

7. BT, June 27, 1900.

John J. Mitchell

8. OG, 1916, pp. 48–65. The Reynolds Club was donated by the widow of Joseph Reynolds (1819–1891), a businessman who engaged variously in milling, tanning, fur-trading, steamship lines, railroads and mining. See *UCB*, Vol. I. Mitchell Tower was the gift of John J. Mitchell (1854–1927), president of the Illinois Trust and Savings Bank and trustee of numerous packing, railway, banking, and utility companies.

9. For the models for these buildings see *An Inventory of the Historical Monuments of the City of Oxford* (England: Royal Commission on Historical Monuments, 1939).

10. Leon Mandel (1841–1911) like MacLeish and Field, was head of one of Chicago's large department stores and active in philanthropic causes. See *UCB*, Vol. II.

Leon Mandel

11. This approach to historicism was defended by Coolidge in his essay on Richardson in which he quotes from Van Rensselaer's biography of Richardson, "it has never been a part of an architect's duty to be original in the absolute meaning of the term. . . . in these late days of art he could not be so even if he tried his best. A process of intelligent adaptation is that which he must employ, and he has a clear title to be called original whenever he perfectly fits old features to new needs and schemes, or so remoulds an old conception that a new conception is the result—not an effective piece of patchwork, but a fresh and vital entity." Charles A. Coolidge, "Henry Hobson Richardson," *Later Years of the Saturday Club, 1870–1920*, ed. M. A. De Wolfe Howe (Boston: Houghton Mifflin Co., 1927), pp. 198–99.

12. In a conference with John C. Olmsted, who was called upon to make a landscape plan, Coolidge articulated his problem in adding to the Cobb buildings. "Coolidge plans History eventually in an L shaped building facing north and west of Walker—proposes to leave a gap of about 10' or 12' wide which may have an arch . . . to tie it to Walker, but he does not want to hitch his somewhat different roof and more refined architectural treatment to Cobb's." Conference between John C. Olmsted and Charles Coolidge, July 22, 1902. Olmsted Papers, Manuscript Division, Library of Congress.

From left: Franklin MacVeagh, President Judson, Ernest DeWitt Burton, Martin A. Ryerson, Charles A. Coolidge, and Charles R. Henderson at Harper Memorial Library dedication, June 1912

CHAPTER 10. CHARLES HITCHCOCK HALL

1. TBG, Jan. 30, 1900. Charles Hitchcock (1827–1891) had been a prominent Chicago lawyer, a Dartmouth classmate and friend of Daniel Shorey, also a lawyer and a trustee of the University from 1892 until his death in 1899. Hitchcock had come

to Chicago in 1854 and in 1860 married Annie McClure and built a home on the corner of 48th and Greenwood Avenue. In 1870 he served as president of the Illinois Constitutional Convention. See *UCB*, Vol. I. Annie McClure Hitchcock (1839–1922) was a founding member of the Fortnightly, Chicago's first women's club devoted to self-education and mutual improvement. See Muriel Beadle et al., *The Fortnightly of Chicago* (Chicago: Henry Regnery and Co., 1973).

2. Mrs. Charles Hitchcock, "Charles Hitchcock Hall," PP 38:12.

3. Dwight Heald Perkins (1846–1941) was born in Memphis, Tennessee, and raised in Chicago. Like Cobb and Coolidge he attended MIT. He worked with Burnham and Root during the Columbian Exposition. In 1897 he designed and built Steinway Hall, where he shared quarters with Robert Spencer, an acquaintance from MIT who had worked with Shepley, Rutan and Coolidge in both Boston and Chicago before starting his own practice. Myron Hunt and Frank Lloyd Wright also shared this office space. These young architects were all in search of a new and indigenous architectural style which later became known as the Prairie School. See H. Allen Brooks, *The Prairie School* (Toronto: University of Toronto Press, 1972); Albert Tannler, "The Creation of Charles Hitchcock Hall 1900–1902," *The University of Chicago Library Society Bulletin*, Vol. I, No. 1, Fall, 1975; National Register of Historic Places Inventory-Nomination Form, Charles Hitchcock Hall; and ABg. See also *The Western Architect, Supplement*, Nov. 1903.

4. Mrs. Charles Hitchcock to Harper, Jan. 31, 1900, PP 38:21.

5. In Dec. 1900, the Committee on Buildings and Grounds resolved that Cobb be requested to consult with the architect for the new dormitory to the end that the building be harmonious.

6. *The Western Architect, Supplement*, Nov. 1903.

7. Mrs. Charles Hitchcock to the workmen and their friends who came to the housewarming of Hitchcock Hall, Oct. 11, 1902, PP 38:21.

Mrs. Charles Hitchcock

CHAPTER 11. QUESTIONING THE STYLE

1. Robert Herrick, "The University of Chicago," *Scribner's Magazine*, Oct., 1895.

2. James Gamble Rogers (1867–1947) graduated from Yale in 1889, then came to Chicago where he worked in the office of William Le Baron Jenney. He left to study at L'Ecole des Beaux-Arts in Paris, returning to Chicago in 1897, where he practiced alone until 1904. In 1904 he went to New York, forming a partnership with Herbert D. Hale of Boston which lasted until 1907. After Hale's retirement Rogers again practiced without associates until 1923 when the firm of James Gamble Rogers, Inc. was formed, and he became architectural adviser to Yale. See Withey, *Biographical Dictionary*.

3. Contract between the Trustees of the Chicago Institute and the University of Chicago, Mar. 5, 1901, PP 19:14.

4. Rogers to Harper, Apr. 12, 1902, PP 10:17.

5. BT, Apr. 25, 1902.

6. *UCB*, Vol. II.

7. Anita McCormick Blaine (1866–1954) was a daughter of the inventor Cyrus McCormick. Widowed when her son was a small boy, she became interested in the progressive education movement, and particularly in the teacher training program of Francis Wayland Parker, whom she sought to release from the restraints of the public educational system to develop his methods in the freedom of a privately supported school. See Gilbert A. Harrison, *A Timeless Affair: The Life of Anita McCormick Blaine* (Chicago: University of Chicago Press, 1979) and Ida B. De Pencier, *The*

John D. Rockefeller, Jr.

History of the Laboratory Schools: The University of Chicago 1896–1965 (Chicago: Quadrangle Books, 1969).

8. For Rogers's discussion of his work on Blaine Hall see James Gamble Rogers, "The Architecture of the School of Education Building," *UR*, VIII, 7, Nov. 1903, pp. 183–86.

9. Henry Holmes Belfield (1837–1912) had been head of the Chicago Manual Training School before it affiliated with the University. He was in charge of the technological course in the high school from 1902 until his retirement in 1908.

10. Blaine to Harper, Mar. 10, 1903, PP 8:23.

11. BT, Sept. 3, 1900. Adolphus Clay Bartlett, a partner in the hardware firm of Hibbard, Spencer, and Bartlett, joined the Board of Trustees in 1900, just after his younger son Frank Dickenson

Adolphus Clay Bartlett

Bartlett had died while vacationing in Europe. A. C. Bartlett was one of Chicago's leading businessmen, active in a number of cultural and philanthropic enterprises. He was a neighbor of Charles Hutchinson on Prairie Avenue. *UCB*, Vol. II.

12. Bartlett to Harper, May 20, 1901, PP 64:20.

13. John D. Rockefeller, Jr., to Harper, June 7, 1901, PP 56:14.

14. Rockefeller, Jr., to MacLeish, June 28, 1901, PP 56:14.

15. MacLeish to Gates, July 6, 1901, FTG 1:16. Lexington Avenue later became University Avenue.

16. BT, July 16, 1901.

17. Memorandum of Interview at Forest Hill, Cleveland, Ohio, Aug. 19, 1901, PP 56:14.

CHAPTER 12. THE PLAN REVISED AND REFINED

1. *UR*, 1901–2, 1902–3.

2. Goodspeed, *History*, pp. 336–38.

3. *PR*, 1892–1902, pp. 266 ff.

4. Minutes of the University Senate, Apr. 7, 1900.

5. *PR*, 1892–1902, pp. 270–71.

6. *PR*, 1892–1902, p. 274.

7. Burton to Harper, Feb. 12, 1903, EDB, Series II, 9:1.

8. Ernest DeWitt Burton (1856–1925) came to the University when it opened as professor of New Testament literature. In 1900 he was made chairman of the Library Commission. From 1910 until his death he was director of the Library. In 1923, following the resignation of President Harry Pratt Judson, he became the third President of the University. See EDB; Thomas W. Goodspeed, *Ernest DeWitt Burton: A Biographical Sketch* (Chicago: University of Chicago Press, 1926); and *Dictionary of American Biography*, Vol. 3.

9. Burton to Harper, Jan. 31, 1903, EDB, Series II, 9:17.

10. Burton to President Taylor at Vassar, Feb. 12, 1903, EDB, Series II, 9:1.

11. EDB, Addenda I.

12. Burton to Parker, Feb. 12, 1903, EDB, Series II, 9:1.

13. The Law School, now Harold Leonard Stuart Hall, designed by Shepley, Rutan and Coolidge, was completed in 1904. It was designed to be large enough to accommodate 1,000 students, but until the Law School grew to that size, the building was expected to house history, political economy, political science, and social science. Harper to Coolidge, Apr. 28, 1902, PP 10:18.

14. Harry Pratt Judson (1849–1927), like Burton, was a member of the first faculty. He was dean of the colleges and professor of history. After the death of President Harper in Jan. 1906, Judson served as Acting President for a year. In Mar. 1907, he became President, a post he held until his resignation in 1923. See *Dictionary of American Biography*, Vol. 10; *UCM*, XIX, 6, Apr. 1927; PP; and ABF.

CHAPTER 13. AN APPROPRIATE SYMBOLISM

1. John Evans and Co. of Boston, the firm that had executed most of Richardson's ornamental work (see O'Gorman, *H. H. Richardson*) and produced the architectural modeling for the Agricultural Building at the Exposition and the Chicago Art Institute, was employed by Coolidge for the Bartlett embellishments, BT, Nov. 5, 1901. Although there is no record, it seems probable that Evans also did the models for the Tower Group and Law School because the company was later engaged to provide the ornament for Harper Library. TBG, Jan. 12, 1910. The company's records are in the archives of the Boston Public Library.

2. TBG, Apr. 10, 1911. John Evans and Co. prepared the model

Julius Rosenwald

for the University seal which was approved by the trustees in Aug. 1910 and adopted in Jan. 1912. The coat of arms, drawn by a Mr. Burke of England, was designed by Pierre de Chaignon La Rose, a Boston heraldist.

3. Money had come to the University for a classics building through the will of Mrs. Elizabeth G. Kelly in 1902. There had been no funds for maintenance, however, so construction was postponed until 1915.

4. Rosenwald Hall, the long-awaited building for geology and geography, was named for its donor, Julius Rosenwald (1852–1932), head of Sears, Roebuck and Co., trustee, and noted philanthropist. For biographical material see M. R. Werner, *Julius Rosenwald: The Life of a Practical Humanitarian* (New York: Harper and Bros., 1939), the Julius Rosenwald Papers, and ABF.

The architects were William Holabird (1865–1923) and Martin Roche (1855–1927), an established Chicago firm dating from the early 1880s. They were known for their design of tall office buildings and hotels. Rosenwald Hall presented special engineering problems, in particular the need for a central concrete pier, rising from bedrock fifty-two feet below city datum, which was constructed to carry seismographic equipment. See T. C. Chamberlin, "Address at the Laying of the Cornerstone of Rosenwald Hall," *UCM*, VI, 8, June 1914. The choice of Holabird and Roche probably reflected a recognition of the firm's expertise in this kind of construction.

5. Ida Noyes Hall, the women's building by Shepley, Rutan and Coolidge, was the gift of La Verne Noyes in memory of his wife. For a life of the donor see *UCB*, Vol. I. For material related to Ida Noyes (1853–1912), see Ida E. S. Noyes, *Occasional Verses, Toasts and Sentiments* (Chicago: La Verne Noyes, 1913), *A Memorial in Honor of Mrs. La Verne Noyes* (Chicago: Chicago Chapter of the Daughters of the American Revolution, 1912), and the Ida Noyes Papers.

6. *UR*, I. n. s. 3, July 1915, pp. 130–31.

7. *UR*, I, n. s. 2, Apr. 1915, pp. 88–90. The sculptor for Rosenwald was Michael Thomas Murphy.

8. See Peter B. Wight, "Three New Buildings at the University of Chicago," *Architectural Record*, XLI, 2, Feb., 1917.

CHAPTER 14. THE UNION OF EXTERIOR AND INTERIOR

1. Joseph Dux, a Chicago architectural sculpture studio, did the interior carving and plaster modeling for the Tower Group and the Law School. BG 33:1; TBG, Aug. 10, 1904. The firm continued to work on University buildings for almost thirty years, preparing the architectural models for the Theology Group (1926), the Medical Group (1927), Wieboldt Hall (1928), Sunny Gym-

nasium and Jones Chemical Laboratory (1929), Eckhart Hall (1930), and Chicago Lying-in Hospital (1931).

2. See Robert Judson Clark, ed., *The Arts and Crafts Movement in America* (Princeton: distributed by Princeton University Press, 1972). There were many ties between the University and the Arts and Crafts movement. In 1897 the Arts and Crafts Society was founded at Hull House which maintained close relationships with the University, particularly through the extension courses offered there. The Art Institute, which counted among its board members Adolphus Clay Bartlett as well as Hutchinson and Ryerson, held its first Arts and Crafts exhibit in 1902. The University community had a flourishing William Morris Society, and Oscar Lovell Triggs, instructor in the English department, was secretary of the Industrial Art League; its board members included President Harper, Professors George Vincent and Emil G. Hirsch, as well as architects Louis Sullivan and Frank Lloyd Wright. See Triggs to Harper, 1899–1904, PP 40: 1. From 1902 to 1904 Marion Talbot wrote a column for *The House Beautiful*, a popular magazine devoted to arts and crafts. MT 7: 6.

3. *UR*, VIII, 6, Oct. 1903, p. 176. Frederick Clay Bartlett (1873–1953) painted a number of murals in Chicago, including those for the Second and Fourth Presbyterian Churches, the Highland Park Trinity Church, the City Hall Council Chamber, and the University Club. For an informal autobiographical sketch see Frederick Clay Bartlett, *Sortofakinda Journal of My Own* (Chicago: F. C. Bartlett, 1965). See also *Friends of American Art Yearbook* (Chicago: 1913–14).

4. *UR*, VIII, 10, Feb. 1904, pp. 316–17.

5. See Alastair Duncan, *Tiffany Windows* (New York: Simon and Schuster, 1980). See also Erne R. Frueh and Florence Frueh, "The Ivanhoe Window," *Stained Glass*, 77, 2, Summer 1982, and Lillian E. Purdy, "Stained Glass in America," PP 10: 17.

6. *UR*, VIII, 10, Feb. 1904, pp. 309–12.

Ida E. S. Noyes

7. *OG*, 1916, p. 60.

8. TBG, June 29, 1903.

9. Richard Bock designed architectural ornament and sculpture for a number of Prairie School architects, including Adler and Sullivan, Frank Lloyd Wright, and George Elmslie.

10. TBG, Sept. 28, 1904.

11. Inventory of Hitchcock Hall, 1919, ABg.

CHAPTER 15. THE SOCIAL VALUE OF TUDOR DOMESTICITY

1. *UR*, II, n. s. 3, July 1916, p. 163.

2. Harper to Ethel Freeman, Sept. 1, 1900, PP 50: 7.

3. TBG, June 16, 1913.

La Verne Noyes

4. Marion Talbot memo on Ida Noyes Hall, PP 50:7.

5. Talbot, *More than Lore*, p. 188.

6. BG 24:12.

7. BG 24:13.

8. Committee on Dedication of Ida Noyes Hall, MT 5:3.

9. BT, Feb. 2, 1918. Jessie Arms Botke was a native Chicagoan who studied at the Art Institute of Chicago. She was a pupil there of Ralph Clarkson, who painted many of the portraits of University faculty and trustees. She worked for interior decorators as a muralist, and later for Albert Herter designing tapestries. She and her husband had a studio in the 57th Street Art Colony. See *UR*, VI, 1, Jan. 1918, pp. 1–6; also BG 24:11.

10. Edith Foster Flint to Judson, Oct. 21, 1916, PP 50: 7.

CHAPTER 16. BURTON'S DEVELOPMENT PROGRAM

1. Burton inherited from Judson an institution that had been financially stabilized. He recognized the virtues of both Harper's and Judson's approach. "President Harper was a daring innovator, a man of creative and constructive and organizing mind, and in the fourteen years that he was President of the University it made a record without equal in the history of American education. President Judson was of a different temper and temperament, but he met the needs of the University as Dr. Harper had met those of an earlier day. In the seventeen years of his administration he gave to it stability and confidence in its future, and he left it not only larger and richer than he found it, but especially established on more solid foundations, its future secure against any storm that is likely to arise." *UR*, n. s. XI, 1, Dec. 1924, pp. 19–20.

2. *UR*, n. s. X, 1, Jan. 1924, p. 19.

3. Ernest D. Burton, *The University of Chicago in 1940* (Chicago: University of Chicago, 1925), p. 52.

4. R. M. Hughes, *A Study of the Graduate Schools of America* (Oxford, Ohio: Miami University, 1925).

5. *UR*, n. s. XV, 2, Apr. 1929, p. 67.

6. Lyman R. Flook's duties as superintendent of construction included writing dockets for the Committee on Buildings and Grounds, working up preliminary designs and estimates, monitoring construction, approving changes, authorizing estimates, and interpreting contracts. BG 27:10.

7. Emery Jackson graduated from the University in 1902. He attended L'Ecole des Beaux-Arts in Paris. He was associated with James Gamble Rogers, and later with Shepley, Rutan and Coolidge. At the time he was asked to be consulting architect for the University he was working in New York as design architect for the Baptist Home Mission Society. He prepared the plans for use in Burton's development campaign, and later was engaged as

a full-time consulting architect, a position he held until 1948. HHS 207: 2.

8. Thomas Elliott Donnelley (1867–1955), president and treasurer of R. R. Donnelley and Sons, served as a trustee from 1909 to 1938, when he became a life trustee. He brought to his chairmanship of the Trustees' Committee on Buildings and Grounds an interest in the fine arts and in printing in particular. The latter made him the ultimate authority on the composition and lettering of all of the building inscriptions and tablets.

9. Harold Higgins Swift (1885–1962) graduated from the University in 1907. He was the son of meat packer Gustavus Swift and became vice-president of the company. He was made a trustee in 1914, the first alumnus to hold that position. In 1922 he became chairman of the Board of Trustees serving until his resignation in 1948. See HHS for a continuous and detailed record of University affairs for the period of his trusteeship.

CHAPTER 17. THE PLAN BROUGHT TO COMPLETION

1. *UR*, n.s. XI, 1, Jan. 1925, pp. 78–79.
2. Harper, *Trend*, p. 58.
3. Mr. and Mrs. Joseph Bond were the parents of Edgar Goodspeed's wife. Mrs. Bond gave the chapel in memory of her husband Joseph Bond (1852–1902), president of the American Radiator Company and a trustee of the Divinity School. See *UCB*, Vol. I.
4. Swift Hall was the gift of Mrs. Gustavus Swift, mother of Harold H. Swift. For a biography of Gustavus F. Swift (1839–1903), founder of Swift and Co., see *UCB*, Vol. I.
5. Professor Harold Willoughby pointed out that its carvings "underscore by contrast the ethical dichotomy between evil and good that Zoroastrianism and Judaism and Christianity have conspicuously insisted on. At the same time they present pictur-

Joseph Bond

esquely the dangers and insecurities outside the religious group in antithesis to the ideal securities within the beloved community." From "Symbolism of Bond Chapel," a talk delivered in Joseph Bond Chapel by Professor Harold R. Willoughby, May 2, 1939, ABg.
6. Charles J. Connick (1875–1945) was born and raised in Pennsylvania. He went to Boston in the early 1900s. An encounter with Ralph Adams Cram, designer of Gothic churches, led to Connick's first commission in the Boston area. Subsequently Connick produced stained glass windows for many of Cram's churches, including the Fourth Presbyterian Church in Chicago. While working in Chicago he met Goodspeed, who was chairman of the committee on the soldier's memorial window for the Hyde Park Baptist Church. They became firm friends and the com-

Mrs. Joseph Bond

dows were installed, a gift from Goodspeed, who worked out their imagery with Connick's successor, Orin Skinner.

8. Describing Wieboldt Hall at the ground-breaking exercises, Professor John Matthews Manly said, "It is to be a laboratory of research in which instructors and students will labor together upon problems of language, of literary history, of criticism, and of interpretation." *UR*, n. s. XII, 1, Jan. 1926, p. 61. Wieboldt Hall was the gift of William A. Wieboldt (1857–1951), merchant, philanthropist, chairman of Wieboldt and Co. Department Store. Born in Germany, he maintained a lifelong interest in its language and culture that led him to offer to fund a building devoted to the modern languages.

The social science building, Professor T. V. Smith said, would

mission for the Baptist church was followed by that for Bond Chapel. Edgar J. Goodspeed, *As I Remember* (New York: Harper and Bros., 1953). For Connick's autobiography, theories about stained glass, and inventory of work, see Charles J. Connick, *Adventures in Light and Color* (New York: Random House, 1937). See also *Stained Glass*, Spring and Autumn, 1946. The Connick records are in the archives of the Boston Public Library.

7. Connick used a variety of symbols and figures to create, in a dazzling mosaic of light, an implied narrative that suggests a comprehensive review of the New Testament. The story begins in the lowest lancets with the kingdom activities of Jesus, continues up to the messages of the apostles and evangelists, and culminates in the apocalyptic vision of St. John, EJG 2:14. See also *The Divinity Student*, Vol. V, 1, Feb. 1928. Connick was always concerned with the interrelationships between windows. A solitary stained glass window could lose its vibrancy under the harsh light of clear windows. After Connick's death his associates continued his work and in 1951 the north, south, and east win-

Harold H. Swift

William A. Wieboldt

be the first, perhaps, in the world "completely equipped for social research, inhabited exclusively by research workers, and devoted entirely to a mastery and control of social process." *UR*, n.s. XV, 2, Apr. 1929, p. 64.

9. Social Science memo, Nov. 16, 1928, BG 29:5.

CHAPTER 18. GOTHIC AND THE DEMANDS OF SCIENCE

1. *UR*, n.s. III, 1, Jan. 1917, pp. 1–7.
2. TBG, Jan. 4, 1918.
3. Hodgdon to Burton, Nov. 22, 1923, PP 11:1.

4. Memorandum of Agreement with Winford Smith, Jan. 20, 1920, BG 23:11.
5. Judson to Ryerson, June 28, 1919, PP 11:1.
6. Smith to Hodgdon, May 4, 1920, PP 11:1.
7. BT, Aug. 9, 1921.
8. BT, Nov. 9, 1921.
9. Memorandum on the Medical Department Situation, Feb. 19, 1922, PP 11:1.
10. Heckman to Burton, Apr. 14, 1923, PP 11:1.
11. Swift to Ryerson, Apr. 4, 1923, PP 11:1.
12. Ryerson to Swift, Apr. 17, 1923, PP 11:1.
13. TBG, Jan. 22, 1925.
14. Coolidge and Hodgdon, Architects, "The Medical Building and Hospital for the University of Chicago," *Architecture*, Jan. 8, 1927, p. 288. See also Coolidge and Hodgdon, Architects and Ralph B. Seem, M.D., "Chicago to Have Notable Medical Education and Hospital Buildings," *The Modern Hospital*, XXVI, 5, May 1926.

CHAPTER 19. MODERN GOTHIC AND THE CHAPEL BLOCK

1. In his letter of designation Rockefeller wrote, "As the spirit of religion should penetrate and control the University, so that building which represents religion ought to be the central and dominant feature of the University group. The Chapel may appropriately embody those architectural ideals from which the other buildings, now so beautifully harmonious, have taken their spirit, so that all the other buildings on the campus will seem to have caught their inspiration from the Chapel and in turn will seem to be contributing their worthiest to the Chapel." John D. Rockefeller to the President and Trustees, Dec. 13, 1910, PP 56:18.

2. Bertram Grosvenor Goodhue (1869–1924) served an appren-

ticeship in James Renwick's office where he went to work at the age of fifteen. He was twenty when he joined the firm of Ralph Adams Cram and Francis Wentworth as head draftsman, later becoming a partner. In 1903 the firm, now Cram, Goodhue and Ferguson, opened a New York office of which Goodhue was head. The partnership was dissolved in 1914. Although Goodhue, Cram, and Ferguson were widely recognized for their Gothic work, Goodhue gradually grew away from his romantic attachment to medievalism. "Contrary to what I suppose is the generally accepted view, I hold no brief for Gothic as opposed to any other style. Gothic seems to be the generally accepted spirit in which churches should be built; also I find its forms attractive, therefore a good deal of Gothic work must be laid to my door; but I assure you I dream of something very much bigger and finer and more modern and more suited to our present-day civilization than any Gothic church could possibly be." Charles Harris Whitaker, ed., *Bertram Grosvenor Goodhue, Architect and Master of Many Arts* (New York: Press of the American Institute of Architects, 1925), p. 27.

3. "Mediaeval Gothic . . . and Modern Gothic, the Gothic of such churches as are being built now all over England and America, are two very distinct things. Mediaeval Gothic is now impossible and must remain mediaeval, and the Gothic we do today, if it is to be vital, and beautiful, and true, and good, and therefore Art, must be of our own times." Ibid., pp. 22–23.

4. Heckman to Goodhue, Aug. 30, 1920, BG 26:12.

5. Goodhue to Ryerson, Jan. 15, 1923, HHS 210:4.

6. Ibid. After Goodhue's death the Committee on Buildings and Grounds ordered a model made by Goodhue Associates with a movable tower so that they could more easily determine where it should be placed. In June, 1925, the committee voted to put the tower on the east side.

7. Burton to Donnelley, Jan. 29, 1924, HHS 210:4.

8. Whitaker, *Goodhue*, p. 29.

9. Burton to Swift, June 19, 1924, HHS 210:4.

10. Burton to Swift, Aug. 18, 1924, HHS 47:6.

11. Report on the Cathedrals of England, HHS 201:1.

12. Max Mason (1877–1961), who became President of the University in Aug. 1925, came from the University of Wisconsin where he had been professor of mathematical physics. He resigned in May 1928, to accept the directorship of the Division of Natural Sciences of the Rockefeller Foundation.

13. Committee on Symbolism to Swift, Mar. 13, 1926, HHS 210:3.

14. Lee Lawrie (1877–1963) was born in Germany but came to America as an infant and was raised in Chicago. He began his career as sculptor in the studios of Augustus Saint Gaudens. From 1908 to 1919 he was instructor in sculpture at Yale. He was regularly employed by Goodhue for sculptural ornament and his work includes the statues for the reredos, St. Thomas Church, New York, the sculpture for the State Capitol Building, Lincoln, Nebraska, the National Academy of Sciences, Washington, D.C., and all of the statues and most of the ornament for the Harkness Memorial Quadrangle at Yale. For Rockefeller Chapel he carved all of the statues up to a height of thirty feet. Above that height the work was executed by Ulric H. Ellerhusen, who had studied first at the Art Institute under Lorado Taft and then at the Art Students League with Gutzon Borglum. Ellerhusen was assisted by Edward Ardolino.

For a complete description of the symbolic sculpture for the chapel, inside and out, see Edgar J. Goodspeed, *The University of Chicago Chapel* (Chicago: University of Chicago Press, 1928).

15. Memo, Jan. 1, 1924, BG 26:14. The ceiling tiles were designed by Hildreth Meiere, who also designed the floors and ceilings of the Nebraska State Capitol.

16. Whitaker, *Goodhue*, p. 27.

17. Memo, Oct. 8, 1928, BG 25:3.

18. Murray to Jackson Sept. 8, 1929, BG 25:3.

19. Lloyd Steere to Breasted Apr. 21, 1930, BG 25:3.

CHAPTER 20. PROBLEMS OF SIZE AND SCALE

1. Memo, Apr. 1, 1925, HHS 208:8.

2. *UR*, n.s. X, 3, June 1924, p. 201.

3. *PR*, 1926–27, p. 3.

4. Revised Memorandum re Dormitory Project, Sept. 27, 1928, BG 12:1.

5. Russell Sturgis, *A Dictionary of Architecture and Building*, 3 vols. (New York: Macmillan and Co., 1901–5), Vol. II, p. 638.

6. C. L. Borie to Jackson, June 10, 1929, BG 12:2. The Philadelphia firm of Zantzinger, Borie and Medary was formed in 1910. Clarence Clark Zantzinger (1872–1951) had graduated from Yale in 1892 and studied architecture at the University of Pennsylvania and L'Ecole des Beaux-Arts. Charles L. Borie, Jr. (1871–1943) was also a graduate of the University of Pennsylvania as was Milton B. Medary (1874–1929). The firm was known for its public and institutional architecture. In addition to its work in various colleges and universities it built hospitals in Philadelphia and Bryn Mawr, the Philadelphia Museum of Art, and the Justice Department building in Washington, D.C. The partners were also involved in planning: Borie was chairman of the Buildings and Grounds Committee at the University of Pennsylvania and Medary was consulting architect to Columbia University and a member of the National Capitol Park and Planning Commission.

7. Preliminary Report of the Committee on New Groups of Residence Halls, Feb. 6, 1929, BG 12:2.

8. Jackson to Borie, Mar. 11, 1930, BG 12:3.

9. Burton-Judson Courts opened at the same time that President Robert Maynard Hutchins's New Plan went into effect, in the fall of 1931. The New Plan called for the abolition of credits, voluntary class attendance, and general examinations to be taken only when the student felt ready. To the extent that the new housing provided for both private work and informal faculty-student interchange it supported the goals of the New Plan, thus giving continuity and confirmation to the views expressed by Harper, Burton, and Woodward that dormitory facilities should serve educational purposes.

10. Edmonds to Jackson, Feb. 14, 1929, BG 20:8.

11. After the death of William Holabird in 1923, and Martin Roche in 1927, John A. Holabird (1886–1945), William's son, and John W. Root (1887–1963), son of Daniel Burnham's partner, assumed control of the firm. Holabird was a graduate of West Point and had studied engineering in the army. He then

Bernard A. Eckhart

went to Paris to study at L'Ecole des Beaux-Arts, where he met John Root, also a student there. Both joined the firm after World War I.

12. Raymond D. Fosdick to George Fairweather, Feb. 27, 1930, BG 20: 8.

13. Holabird and Root to Fairweather, Mar. 14, 1930, BG 20: 8.

14. For a detailed description of the interior see *The Hotel Monthly*, Vol. 40, No. 477, Dec. 1932.

15. Smith to Heckman, Oct. 5, 1931, BG 21: 3.

CHAPTER 21. THE PERSISTENCE OF SYMBOLISM

1. BT, Dec. 10, 1925.

2. List of models for Wieboldt Hall executed in accordance with instructions from J. M. Manly, Nov. 19, 1926, BG 34: 6.

3. TBG, Jan. 29, 1929.

4. Report of the Committee on Symbolism for the New Mathematics Building, BG 16: 8. The donor of Eckhart Hall was Bernard A. Eckhart (1852–1931), manufacturer and president of B. A. Eckhart Milling Co. He held various public posts including: member of the Illinois Senate, 1887–9, trustee of the Chicago Sanitary District, 1891–1900, and president of the West Chicago Park Commission, 1905–8.

The architect was Charles Z. Klauder (1872–1938), a specialist in collegiate architecture. He had a national reputation for college buildings in the Gothic style and served as architect and adviser for Princeton, Pennsylvania State, and the University of Pittsburgh. With Herbert C. Wise he was author of *College Architecture in America* (New York: C. Scribner's Sons, 1929).

5. The new chemistry building was the gift of George Herbert Jones (1856–1941), retired president of Inland Steel. The architects were Coolidge and Hodgdon.

George Herbert Jones

6. The architectural models for the ornamentation on this building were by Joseph Dux, a firm the University had been using since 1903. The models for the portrait heads were by Marie Wishart of Lorado Taft's Midway Studios. TBG, Aug. 5, 1928.

7. Franklin McLean to Carl Erikson, Nov. 4, 1929, BG 14: 5.

8. International House Symbolism, Mar. 28, 1932, ABg. The models for these carvings were made by J. M. Jonson and Alvin Meyer, of Holabird and Root's sculpture studio.

9. *The Oriental Institute News and Notes*, No. 45, Dec. 1978.

CHAPTER 22. MINIMAL GOTHIC AND THE FIELD HOUSE

1. *The Program for Athletic Development at The University of Chicago*, Nov. 1924, BG 17: 4.

2. Donnelley to Ryerson, June 17, 1925, BG 17:4.

3. TBG, July 14, 1925.

4. TBG, Sept. 1, 1925.

5. TBG, Sept. 10, 1925.

6. *UCM*, XXIV, 3, Jan. 1932, p. 131.

7. *UR*, n.s. XIII, 3, July, 1927, pp. 225–26.

EPILOGUE: A CENTURY OF PROGRESS AND THE DEMISE OF GOTHIC

1. Robert Morss Lovett, "Progress—Chicago Style," *Current History*, Vol. 39, 1933–34, p. 434.

2. Robert Maynard Hutchins (1899–1977) served as President of the University from 1929 to 1945 and Chancellor from 1945 to 1951. He attended Oberlin College for two years, served in the ambulance corps in World War I, and finished his undergraduate education at Yale, after which he attended the Yale Law School. He was dean of the Yale Law School before coming to the University. During his first years as President of the University he took the results of a ten-year study by faculty committees and put the recommendations into effect, bringing about a restructuring of the University's educational program and administration. See Presidents' Papers 1925–45 and Robert Maynard Hutchins Papers.

3. Floyd W. Reeves, Nelson B. Henry, John Dale Russell, *The University of Chicago Survey* (Chicago: University of Chicago Press, 1933), Vol. XI, p. 121.

4. Ibid., p. 127.

5. Memo of conversation with Martin A. Ryerson, Oct. 30, 1923, PP 51:8.

6. TBG, June 4, 1929.

7. Jackson to Steere, July 28, 1931, HHS 207:17.

8. For an account of the University's building program subsequent to 1932 see Calvert W. Audrain, William B. Cannon, and Harold J. Wolff, "A Review of Planning at the University of Chicago, 1891–1978," *UR*, XII, 4, Apr. 1978. For a photographic presentation of interiors and exteriors of University buildings, 1892–1976, see D. J. R. Bruckner and Irene Macauley, eds., *Dreams in Stone* (Chicago: R. R. Donnelley and Sons Company, 1976).

APPENDIX A. LANDSCAPING BY OLMSTED BROTHERS

1. *PR*, 1892–1902, p. 1.

2. TBG, Apr. 3, 1901.

3. John Charles Olmsted (1852–1920) was the nephew of Frederick Law Olmsted, who, after the death of his brother, married his sister-in-law and adopted her young family. After getting a degree from the Sheffield Scientific School at Yale in 1875, John C. Olmsted entered Frederick Law Olmsted's landscape office in New York City. In 1884, following the move of the office to Brookline, Mass., John C. Olmsted became a full partner in the firm. After Frederick Law Olmsted retired, in 1898, John C. and Frederick, Jr., formed the Olmsted Bros. firm. During the first quarter of the twentieth century they had an extensive practice, designing parks and campuses across the United States.

4. Olmsted Papers, Manuscript Division, Library of Congress.

5. Olmsted Bros. Report to the Trustees, Mar. 20, 1902, CBT 3:3.

6. Hutchinson and Ryerson, both of whom employed Olmsted to landscape their Lake Geneva estates, asked Olmsted to prepare a plan for Yerkes Observatory that would utilize their surplus plant material. For the Yerkes Observatory landscape plan see Olmsted Papers, Manuscript Division, Library of Congress.

7. For specifications for the pond see BG 2:1. See also John M. Coulter to Harper, Feb. 16, 1904, CBT 3:7.

DATE DUE

ILL
9-30-92
ILL
11-24-96

DEMCO 38-297

Printing ... initials in Michaelangelo. ... by Halliday Lithography. The University of Chicago

The University seal, adopted by the trustees in 1912, was designed by the Boston firm, John Evans and Company, architectural sculptors for Shepley, Rutan and Coolidge.